THE WI COOKBOOK

THE WI COOKBOOK

THE FIRST 100 YEARS

MARY GWYNN

EBURY
PRESS

1915

2015

'If a census of opinion was taken it would probably be found that what members value most is the friendship, the fun, the give and take, and the fellowship that comes from belonging to an Institute.'

Fruit canning demonstration to WI members,
1940s

Introduction

*'The WI is for all women
and it's totally great.'*

India Knight

In an issue of the Women's Institute's own magazine *Home & Country* from 1935, Florence White, founder of the English Folk Cookery Association and author of the recently published and much praised regional cookery book *Good Things in England* (still in print today), wrote: *'It has been said with truth that the history of civilisation could be written from the point of view of food and cookery.'*

Where it all began

The story of the Women's Institute has had food and cookery at its heart from the outset. When newly widowed Madge Watt arrived from Canada to live in Britain in early 1913, this indomitable lady found a country ready and waiting for a new movement dedicated to the needs of women in a rapidly changing society. Drawing on her experience as founder member of the first WI to be established in British Columbia, Madge spoke at a conference in London on the important role countrywomen could take in growing more food to support the war effort. As archivist Anne Stamper observed: 'Rural communities were emerging from a long period of decline, there was a world war ... home farms assumed a new importance. At the same time, the women's suffrage movement was making everyone ... evaluate the role of women and their position in society.' Madge's words resonated with the country's women, and the first Women's Institute was set up in September 1915 in the Anglesey village of Llanfairpwll, with a programme concentrating on food production.

'The WI gives you an opportunity to learn something you didn't know or couldn't do yesterday.' Marchwood WI member

In 1917 the National Federation of Women's Institutes (NFWI) was born. The first Chairman was Lady Gertrude (Trudie) Denman, an extraordinarily modern woman and a major figure in the movement's rapid development, who would imbue and inspire the new WI with her own drive, confidence and strength of character. New Vice Chairman Grace Hadow wrote at the time: 'The WI is for all alike: rich and poor, gentle and simple, learned and unlearned ... each acts in turn as hostess to her fellow members, each puts her own experience and her own practical knowledge at the service of the rest.' By the end of the First World War in 1918 there were 700 WIs; only a year later this number had doubled. Women had emerged from the war with a new confidence and, for those over 30, the vote. The WI encouraged them to take a bigger role in the life and work of rural communities, to support and work for regeneration as part of the post-war effort, most particularly through the medium of education. And, as Anne Stamper concluded in her paper: 'The WI's role to provide for the educational and social needs of

Top image
Wartime jam factory,
1940

Bottom image
Wartime fruit canning,
1940

'Forget the stereotype associated with the WI; it doesn't matter what age you are or what you're interested in, there's likely to be something on offer for you.' **Seven Hills WI member**

━━━━━━━━━━━━━ ●⚬ ⦚⚬⦚ ⚬● ━━━━━━━━━━━━━

members ... is still relevant today.' The WI was, and still is, in essence a feminist movement in the true sense of the word.

A modern movement

Current Chair, charismatic Janice Langley, reiterated all of this in her welcoming speech at a series of 'Inspiring Women Working Together' conferences held for members around the country in early 2014. Speaking at Ascot Racecourse to an enthusiastic audience of 500 Presidents and members from across the South East, Janice paid tribute to the energy of those present and welcomed the increasing membership of the movement. She promised that 'the modern WI gives all kinds of opportunities for all kinds of women'. The key messages Janice and the current NFWI Board of Trustees wanted to get across to members revealed the prevailing attitude within the organisation – 'The WI will inspire you but it's what you make it, and it can be everything you want it to be.' Despite what some commentators might see as evidence to the contrary, the modern WI is definitely not stuck in a stereotypical blue-rinse, Jam and Jerusalem, country backwater. Ever flexible and responsive to the needs of its members and British society, in the 21st Century the WI is still here to provide inspiration, friendship and fun – to give women a voice in their community and beyond it. This organisation exists for, and because of, its members, and as Janice was implicitly saying: 'It's up to you, ladies,' – there are no excuses for ignoring the opportunities that the WI has always prided itself in offering women.

Friendship and new skills are at the heart of what the WI provides. And a welcoming cup of tea and a slice of home-baked cake has always been an integral part of any WI meeting since the first one in Anglesey in 1915 – still very much the case in 2015. Members pride themselves on their baking – and might argue that The Great British Bake Off is merely riding on the coat-sleeves of WI members! Recipes, once handed on by word of mouth or written on scraps of paper or on the back of envelopes, may now be more likely to be exchanged online, but the secrets of a perfect Victoria sponge or jar of lemon curd are likely to be just as hotly debated at meetings, alongside such topical issues of the day as the threat posed by climate

————— ∘◦ ⦂◦⦂ ◦∘ —————

change, concerns about lack of midwives, and the issue of food waste. The WI has always been prescient in its campaigning, involving members from ground level up with the topical concerns of the day, often well ahead of national awareness.

The state of the nation's cooking skills has always been important to a movement dedicated to educating its members to look after themselves. WI publications, from magazines to pamphlets and books of all descriptions, have had a place in many a British kitchen (and beyond) over the century. The last decade has witnessed cookery books moving out of the kitchen to the coffee or bedside table (a recent report showed that despite the modern obsession with cookery books and programmes, the most frequently eaten meal at home is the sandwich), but even in the new digital age WI recipes, whether from books, website or via social media, still have a role to play in imparting wisdom.

Back in 1975 Bee Nilson was the experienced and assured editor of the last major WI cookbook published to celebrate an important anniversary. At 225 pages, The *WI Diamond Jubilee Cookbook* contained no photography but over 500 simple recipes sourced from cookery books produced by WI members across England and Wales. This traditional publication was broken into an established chapter format – soups and starters, fish, meat, cakes, quick breads and scones and so forth, and in her one-page introduction, Bee explained her methods for recipe selection: to reflect the great variety of tastes amongst members, to celebrate regional differences, and even because she was intrigued by the names of some of the dishes. But, most of all, she cites the importance of these recipes as a national record. As she says: 'WI members have been preserving traditional recipes, not as museum pieces but as practical recipes for modern cooks.'

————— ∘◦ ⦂◦⦂ ◦∘ —————

Women in the Community campaign 'to put the WI in its rightful place on the map of contemporary Britain' was launched at the NFWI AGM, 1984

Forty years on, the cookery world and the arena the WI operates in have changed beyond recognition, and the 100th anniversary of the organisation provides the perfect opportunity to produce a cookery book that does what Bee was aiming to do – provide practical, fail-safe recipes for everyday cooks operating in the new millennium. However, it also offers an ideal chance to provide current members of the WI with a wonderful illustration of their organisation's rich history, through the medium of a cookery book. And at the same time, to introduce the WI, its history, wisdom and also its relevance, to those who may be unaware of the fascinating background story of the movement, not only cooks of all levels but also those interested in the social history of our countryside. For, as the reader will discover, the WI has been at the heart of much that has happened to change and develop this country over the last momentous 100 years, particularly, but not exclusively, for women.

'Since its beginnings The Women's Institute has been renowned for its vigorous campaigning. You have been ahead of the time on a whole host of issues including equal pay, breast cancer screening, and banning smoking in public places. The issues you fight for are not always the most glamorous. But you have a formidable reputation for standing your ground and showing just what can be achieved when people come together to get things done.'
Theresa May MP, Home Secretary, July 2014

⸻ ❖ ⸻

And today with a new lease of life, the WI is where it should be – supporting women in their day-to-day lives. As Jane Robinson says in her 2011 book, *A Force to be Reckoned With*: 'The WI has to adapt and go with the (frenetic) flow.' Always flexible, redoubtable (and luckily always able to take a joke, even if at its own expense!), the WI is going from strength to strength. This book is a celebration of the organisation from its inauguration to the present day. It is back where it belongs – at the heart of society.

How to use this book

There are several ways to approach this publication. Use it for its primary purpose as a cookery book and you will find simple and delicious recipes, many for traditional home-cooked dishes that have appeared in WI publications and formed the backbone of British cooking over a century. Try the recipes in their original form for a step back in time to how our grandmothers and mothers cooked, and discover the tastes of a different age. Note that many of these recipes have been transposed exactly as they first appeared, so you may find methods or ingredients unfamiliar. Or try one of the modern versions, all brought up to date for 21st century sensibilities, and carefully tested. As many as possible of these alternative recipes have been sourced from WI archives, and I have drawn attention to any changes made to reflect modern tastes. Whichever you choose, don't mix and match as weights and measures have been worked out separately. Unless you are confident, only work with one version.

You might just decide to take the book to bed with you and read the recipes with their introductions for a fascinating and revealing perspective on their time. You'll soon discover that the way the recipes are written reflects the wisdom and attitudes of each decade. It's so easy for us to either be sniffy about what has gone before or to treat it with too much reverence. The voices that speak through these pages of recipes show common sense and reflect their time perfectly. Let's not dismiss their knowledge by considering them quaint. They can help us re-evaluate our own attitudes to food and its place in society.

*Left to right: top line
WI delegates at the
NFWI AGM, 1922*

*Wartime fruit preserving,
1943*

*Large image bottom left
Mereworth jam centre,
1943*

*HM The Queen visits
Denman College, 1979*

*WI float in the Lord
Mayor's Show, 1947*

1915–1925

1915 The formation of the WI by Margaret (Madge) Watt

1918 Women over 30 get the vote

1919 First woman MP, Nancy Astor, takes her seat in Parliament in 1919, followed by WI member Margaret Winteringham in 1921 – known as our 'institute member'

1919 Lewes WI opens the first WI market in December

1923 Bill passed making it easier for women to petition for divorce

1924 Jerusalem sung at WI meetings for the first time

1926–1935

1926 General strike

1928 Women over 21 get the vote

1928 WI recognised for vital role in educating country women

1929 First Green Belt area approved near Hendon

1929 Black Thursday – US stock market crashes

1930 In 1930 there are 291,570 WI members

1930 The WI in discussions with the government to set up more markets around the country

1936–1945

1936 Death of George V and the abdication crisis

1936 WI campaigns for better nutrition

1938 All Britons measured for gas masks

1938 Lady Denman becomes director of the Women's Land Army

1939 The Second World War

1943 Part time war work made compulsory in 1943 for women aged 18–45

1946–1955

1948 Denman College opens

1948 NHS begins 'care from cradle to grave'

1948 First fully self-service 'supermarket' opens (Co-op)

1948 Formation of WIs in the Channel Islands

1948 End of clothes rationing; 1950 petrol, and finally all rationing in 1954

1950 In 1950 there are 446,675 WI members (the peak for membership)

1953 The Queen's Coronation

1954 Death of Lady Denman

1956–1965

1957 Creation of the Common Market

1958 The M1 is opened – the first motorway in Britain

1958 Cambridge WI members form a new WI in Fulbourne Mental Hospital

1960 End of National Service

1960 First woman prime minister elected in Ceylon, in 1960

1960 The Kremlin invites Gabrielle Pike, NFWI Chair, to visit

1961 Contraceptive pill goes on sale in the UK

1965 First woman High Court Judge in the UK

WI resolutions include action to combat venereal disease and humane slaughter of animals

WI resolutions include issue of maternal mortality in childbirth, and a campaign to support the establishment of rural libraries

WI resolutions include issue of equal pay for women, and the setting up of a WI college

WI resolutions include food production and healthy eating in times of shortage, and every village to have a doctor's surgery

WI resolutions include nationwide publicity for the dangers of spreading foot-and-mouth disease, the issue of the danger of radiation on future generations and a campaign for the facilities to provide routine smear tests for cervical cancer

1966–1975	1976–1985	1986–1995	1996–2005	2006–2015
1967 BBC starts broadcasting in colour	**1976** After the worst inflation since the organisation was set up, the NFWI introduces annual subscription	**1986** First cow infected with BSE to die in UK confirmed	**1996** WI undertakes research into pensions, revealing the true unpaid caring work of women and that almost 90% of women know nothing about pensions	**2006** *WI Life* magazine is launched to replace *Home & Country*
1967 Britain's first anti-litter week takes place		**1987** The Great Storm lashes Britain		**2008** World financial crisis
1968 Assassination of Martin Luther King in 1968		**1987** Black Monday – world stock markets crash in October		**2009** WI Cookery School opened at Denman College
1969 The first moon landing	**1979** Margaret Thatcher becomes Britain's first woman Prime Minister	**1989** Collapse of the Berlin Wall	**2000** In 2000 there are 220,000 WI members	**2010** *Voices of the WI* album launched
1971 Decimal currency introduced	**1980** In 1980 there are 384,288 WI members	**1990** In 1990 there are 291,570 WI members		**2011** Default retirement age scrapped, and retirement ages equalised
1971 The Queen Mother opens the Teaching Centre at Denman College	**1981** Unemployment reaches 2.5 million in the UK	**1990** Nelson Mandela released after 27 years in prison	**2000** Tony Blair addresses the WI Triennial General Meeting	**2012** The Queen celebrates her Diamond Jubilee
1973 The miners' work-to-rule movement leads to the three-day working week	**1982** Argentina invades the Falkland Islands	**1992** WI becomes a founder member of the Fairtrade Foundation	**2000** The dot-com bubble inflates and bursts	
1973 Britain joins the EEC (the NFWI held a conference on the Common Market in 1970)	**1982** First BBC Food and Drink programme broadcast	**1993** Recession leads to unemployment of nearly 3m	**2001** Foot-and-mouth outbreak in the UK	**2012** The UK hosts the London 2012 Olympics
	1985 Live Aid concert held at Wembley		**2001** World Trade Center in New York destroyed	**2012** Launch of WI foods including jams, flours and biscuits
			2003 *Calendar Girls* film released	
WI resolutions include free family planning, and a campaign for a national policy on reclamation, recycling and reuse of waste	WI resolutions include overuse and pollution of marine life, and in light of the problem of underage drinking campaign, for the government to promote education in schools, homes and clubs on the dangers of alcohol	WI resolutions urge the government to review the Obscene Publications Act to help the courts deal with violent and explicit content, and campaign for local and global sustainable development	WI resolutions include human trafficking, especially of women and children, and concerns about the increase in obesity and diet-related health problems in children	WI resolutions include the call for more midwives, fighting the closure of post offices, and an SOS for honeybees and pollinators

WI members at the first WI meeting in
Llanfairpwll on Anglesey in Wales,
16 September 1915

1915–1925
Breaking down barriers

Four years after the establishment of the WI in the UK, as the country returned to peace, March 1919 saw the publication of the very first issue of the organisation's own magazine, *Home & Country*. A letter in the first issue from 'The Editors' called the publication 'a grave financial undertaking', and requested readers to 'send your best recipes'. Still sent out regularly to members today under the title *WI Life*, early issues of the magazine (priced at 2d) provided everything from reports from institutes and federations across the country and news of up and coming WI events, to household advice and cooking tips. The magazine carried both national and classified advertising, which give us as many clues to the issues and concerns of the day.

Mrs Hooper of Pershore WI, in what was only the fourth issue of the magazine, wrote: 'It has been said that no women's gathering is complete or satisfactory without tea.' But, as she was at pains to point out, it is 'not necessarily greediness that makes us all so fond of "the cup that cheers".' Then, as is still the case at WI meetings today, tea-time was viewed as the ideal opportunity 'for members to make each other's acquaintance' and, what is more, 'break down social barriers'. The hope was, that with the end of the war, food would become more plentiful and that WI teas, the mainstay of every meeting, could be hosted by groups of members – either four, six or eight depending on the size of the local membership. Mrs Hooper goes on: 'I'm sure you will agree that it is extremely undesirable' that tea should be given by 'one or two of the richer members, which is a form of patronizing, which the best women of all classes hate'.

From the outset the aims of the WI were clear. As a movement, it was determined to welcome all comers to its meetings, and the social aspect was as important as the desire to give women a proper forum to develop their role in society. Lady Denman wrote in the opening issue of *Home & Country* that 'village will be united with village and county with county'. The war and the privations that the country

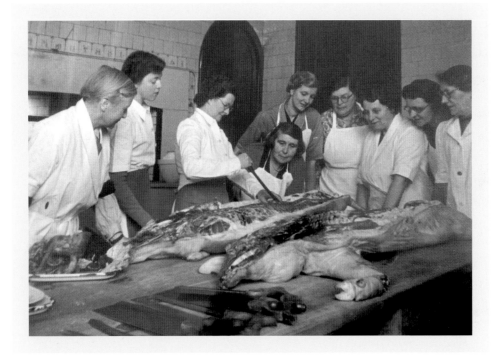

went through served to confirm women's vital role at the heart of rural communities, and the WI was determined to become 'a permanent part of the rural life of the country'. In October 1917, with rumours circulating that there were only three weeks' food supply left in the country, members were urged 'to take every opportunity of becoming more skilled... in the production of food'. Initiatives were set up to re-establish old crafts in order to provide a livelihood for village women, and the first WI market opened in Lewes in 1919. By 1921, it was selling produce from 23 local WIs.

Education was also made a priority as members urged county councils to develop adult education in rural areas – so much so that lobbying from WI members saw more than 18 counties set up rural library schemes.

Top image
Lady Denman, 1923

Bottom image
Wartime jam canning, 1940s

Fresh Lemonade

This simple recipe appears in one of the very earliest issues of Home & Country *magazine from June 1919, as part of a response to a request from members for 'cooling summer drinks'. Food preparation tips, alongside sourcing and cooking advice, played a key role in the magazine during this period and 'Helpful Household Hints!' or 'H. H. H.!' appear regularly through the magazine's first decade.*

Remember that in 1919, fridges, though invented in the previous century, were not a standard feature of the kitchen. In fact many country kitchens would not have electricity until well after the next war, so every cook faced the ever-present challenge to keep food fresh and palatable.

Makes 1 litre · Preparation 15 minutes, plus soaking

175g granulated sugar
1.5 litres cold water
3 lemons
sprigs of fresh mint (optional)

1 Place the sugar in a pan with 500ml of the water and heat gently without boiling until the sugar dissolves. Bring to the boil and simmer for 5-7 minutes until you have a thin syrup. Squeeze the lemons and strain the juice through a sieve. Pour the hot syrup over the squeezed lemon rinds and leave to soak for 2 hours.

2 Add the strained juice to the rinds with the remaining litre of water. Line a sieve with a clean piece of muslin and use to strain the lemonade (or use a jelly bag) to produce a clear drink. Serve chilled or poured over crushed ice with a sprig of fresh mint if desired. Store in a covered jug in the fridge.

'The opportunity to meet new friends, learn new things and be part of an iconic organisation like the WI is just too good to miss.' **WIGs member**

Lemonade from fresh lemons

It is a well-known fact that 'lemon juice' is a potent enemy to disease germs. It has been said by some medical men that nothing is better to prevent catching some diseases which are rife than to... rinse one's mouth with the juice of a lemon. This is especially applicable to hot dusty days when one returns home feeling (to use a vulgarism) grubby!

Ingredients: *1 quart water, ¾ lb sugar, 6 lemons, 2 quarts water.*

Method: *Boil the sugar with the quart of water. Remove the juice from the lemons and pour the syrup over the rinds. Allow these to soak for about two hours. Add the strained juice of the lemons to this and the two quarts of water. Pass through a muslin or jelly bag to clear and serve in glass jugs. This makes about seven pints of lemonade. N.B. A small piece of ice to each glass is a great improvement.*

Rosehip Jelly

Rosehips have been a ready source of vitamins for countrywomen to preserve for their families for generations. In a later WI publication, Wines, Syrups and Cordials, *the reader is advised that 'a dessertspoonful of rosehip syrup a day is the recommended dose'. Nowadays rosehips would probably be classed as a 'super food', as their antioxidant properties rival those of the much-hyped blueberry. Their importance as a source of vitamin C is demonstrated by the regular appearance of members' rosehip recipes in early issues of* Home & Country. *Readers were advised to gather the hips around the end of October when quite ripe but before any frosts. The updated recipe for rosehip jelly has been adapted from* WI Home Skills: Preserves and Preserving.

Makes 2.7kg · Preparation 25 minutes, plus leave overnight · Cook 20 minutes

2kg cooking apples, washed
    and cut up (no need to peel)
1kg rosehips, washed and
    coarsely chopped
granulated sugar

1 Place the apples in a pan with enough cold water to cover completely. Bring to the boil and cook gently until soft and mushy. Add the minced rosehips to the pan and simmer gently for 10–15 minutes. Tip the pulp into a jelly bag suspended over a basin so it doesn't touch it at all and leave to drip overnight.

2 The next day measure the juice. For every 600ml add 500g sugar. Warm the sugar and put in a preserving pan with the juice. Heat gently to dissolve the sugar. Bring to the boil and boil rapidly until setting point is reached (see page 86).

Rosehip marmalade

*Home & Country
1919*

ANSWERS TO LAST MONTH'S QUERY
Gather hips about October, and to every pound of fruit allow ½ pint of water, boil until soft then strain through a sieve. To each 1 lb of pulp allow 1 lb of sugar, boil for thirty minutes, add some chopped preserved ginger just before removing marmalade from fire. - Miss Elba Hayden, Netherhampton.

Stovies

The WI was established in Scotland separately in 1917, as the Scottish Women's Rural Institutes, but many exiled Scots were active members of their local WI across the rest of the UK. Stoved potatoes, or stovies, are the Scottish version of what most British homes would serve up on a Monday after Sunday's roast dinner. Leftovers, maybe bulked out with extra potatoes and fried or baked, became bubble and squeak in England, boxtie, colcannon or champ (see page 152) in Ireland.

From its inception the WI had been debating whether to set up separate institutes for men or simply to include them in meetings, and the same issue of Home & Country *that carried this recipe for potatoes, also had a report on a questionnaire sent out about the need for men's institutes. Later that year the AGM saw a controversial resolution 'on the advisability of bringing men... into the ...movement', voted down.*

Serves 4 · Preparation 10 minutes · Cook 50 minutes

1 tbsp lard or beef dripping

2 medium onions, finely chopped

1kg potatoes, peeled and thickly sliced

300ml meat stock or leftover gravy, plus extra if needed

salt and freshly ground pepper

leftover meat and vegetables (optional)

1   Preheat the oven to 190°C/fan oven 170°C/Gas mark 5. Heat the lard or dripping (you can use the fat from the joint) in a large flameproof casserole on a medium heat. Add the onions and cook for 5–8 minutes until soft but not browned. Add any leftover meat, shredded into small pieces.

2   Add the potatoes in layers, seasoning each layer with salt and pepper as you go. Pour over the stock or gravy. Cover and cook in the oven for 45–50 minutes, checking from time to time to make sure the stock isn't boiling dry. If it is, add a little extra stock. Add any leftover vegetables 10 minutes before the end of cooking, stir well and check the seasoning; cover and cook for a further 10 minutes until the potatoes are tender. The finished dish should be quite moist. Stovies are traditionally served with oatcakes.

Stoved potatoes (a Scotch recipe)

Home & Country
1919

Peel and slice potatoes. Put in a saucepan with a little water, a large sliced onion, pepper and salt to taste, and a tablespoonful of beef dripping. Cook very slowly, about forty minutes, and serve very hot. Cabbage cut up finely can be added if liked.

Vegetarian Pudding

Vegetarianism grew in popularity in Great Britain in the early 20th century as a result of concerns over animal welfare, economic and nutrition issues, and the publicity surrounding famous practitioners at the time such as Mahatma Gandhi and George Bernard Shaw. Many of the suffragettes were vegetarian, too.

This recipe appeared in Home & Country *magazine's Helpful Handy Hints alongside a suggestion for Savoury Cutlets (cooked rice and potatoes flavoured with herbs, shaped and deep-fried in breadcrumbs to look like meat). In lean times it was the practice for women to serve up any precious meat to the working man of the house while she and the children ate meat-free versions. Our updated recipe bakes rather than steams the savoury pudding and serves it with a fresh tomato sauce to keep a similar flavour combination to the original. You can also add other grated root vegetables such as beetroot or swede.*

Serves 4 · Preparation 15 minutes · Cook 45–50 minutes

150g self-raising flour
75g butter or margarine
2 tbsp each chopped flat-leaved
   parsley and fresh thyme
1 medium onion, finely chopped
2 large old potatoes, such as
   King Edwards, cooked
   and mashed
2 large carrots, scrubbed
   and grated
1 large parsnip, peeled
   and grated
1–2 tbsp sun-dried tomato paste
2 large free-range eggs, beaten
2–3 tablespoons milk
5 tbsp freshly grated Parmesan
salt, freshly ground black
   pepper and a large pinch
   of cayenne

1   Preheat the oven to 180°C/fan oven 160°C/gas mark 4. Sift the flour into a large mixing bowl and rub in the fat. Stir in the herbs, onion and vegetables and plenty of seasoning. Whisk together the tomato paste, eggs and milk and use to bind the pudding, adding half the Parmesan.

2   Spoon the mixture into a buttered 1 litre shallow dish, scatter with the remaining Parmesan and bake for 45–50 minutes until risen and golden brown. Serve with a fresh tomato sauce.

Home & Country
1920

Vegetarian pudding

Take 2 large carrots, wash and scrape them on a bread-grater, 3 cold potatoes, a breakfast cup of flour into which rub 3 to 4 ozs. of margarine: then add a packet of tomato soup powder and pepper and salt with a tablespoonful of chopped thyme and parsley; a small onion may be added if liked, mix well together with milk and steam for two hours. 1 egg is a great improvement.

Kedgeree

Adapted from kichri, a humble Indian lentil and rice dish, and brought back to this country by the British Raj, kedgeree was enjoyed by the Victorians and Edwardians as an essential part of their sumptuous breakfasts. Eliza Acton wrote a recipe for it in 1845, and hers was one of the first examples to include eggs. This recipe, sent in response to Home & Country *magazine's editor's plea for properly tested recipes, is simple in its approach but includes key ingredients we still recognise today. With a little enhancement, it is an excellent simple supper served with a salad. Make it with good-quality smoked haddock and buy a top brand curry paste for a well-balanced flavour.*

Serves 4 · Preparation 15 minutes · Cook 35 minutes

350g smoked haddock fillet
50g butter
1 bunch spring onions, sliced
1 clove garlic, crushed
1 tbsp good-quality medium
   curry paste
200g basmati rice
3 tbsp chopped flat-leaved
   parsley
juice of ½ lemon
4 tbsp single cream
2 hard-boiled eggs, shelled
   and chopped
salt, freshly ground black
   pepper and a large pinch
   of cayenne

1 Place the haddock in a wide shallow pan and pour over 650ml cold water to just cover the fish. Bring to the boil and simmer very gently for 8–10 minutes until the flesh is firm and flakes easily. Lift the fish out of the water and flake the flesh, removing any skin. Keep the fish warm and reserve the cooking liquid.

2 Heat half the butter in a heavy-based pan and add the onions and garlic. Cook very gently for 5 minutes until soft, then stir in the curry paste and cook for a minute. Add the rice and stir to coat in the juices. Pour in 450ml of the fish cooking liquid, bring to the boil, then cover the pan and simmer gently for 20 minutes until the rice is just tender.

3 Fork through the flaked fish, remaining butter, parsley, lemon juice and seasoning. Drizzle over the cream and top with the chopped eggs, then cover the pan and leave to stand for 5 minutes. Serve with a salad.

Home & Country
1920

Kedgeree

Boil 8 oz of rice as for curry, that is cooked for fourteen minutes in fast boiling water. Drain and mix with 1 lb flaked fish, a bit of butter, a tea-cup of milk, or, of [sic] possible, cream. Season with pepper and a shake of Cayenne, stir over the fire till very hot, and serve on a dish with the grated yoke [sic] of an egg sprinkled over.

Ginger Cake

Sixty years on from the publication of her Book of Household Management, *Mrs Beeton's eponymous* Family Cookery, *with more than 3,000 recipes, was required reading for many newly-weds learning to manage in a new home. Aimed squarely at the middle-class housewife, a new issue revised and printed after the war reflected the changing times. Its introduction commended 'The art of "using-up" – the cry and the need for economy is greater today than ever'.*

Mrs Beeton advised the baker of cakes that needed sugar as follows: 'Refined sugar can be procured at so low a price, already ground and pulverized that it is more economical to buy than ... loaf sugar'. For a ginger cake, however, she advises choosing the 'coarsest brown sugar'. This recipe uses neither but opts for treacle instead. It is made without fat or eggs, producing more of a biscuit than what we would recognise as a cake. But it is the first appearance in Home & Country *magazine of a spice that holds a dear place at the heart of the WI.*

The updated recipe for a traditional ginger Yorkshire Parkin (over the page) – a recipe with countless WI versions – is adapted from the Yorkshire Federation of WIs Seven Hundred Recipes.

Home & Country
1920

Ginger cake

Ingredients: *1 cup of flour, 1 teaspoon of ground ginger, 1 teaspoonful of ground spice, ½ cup of treacle, ½ cup of milk, 1 teaspoonful of carbonate of soda, 1 tablespoonful of lukewarm water.*

Method: *Mix dry ingredients together, dissolve the soda in the water, add to the treacle and milk, heat all to a smooth batter and bake in a well-greased shallow tin for twenty five to thirty minutes in a moderate oven. This cake will keep moist for several days.*

Yorkshire Parkin

Rather than provide a more modern recipe for an alternative to the 1920's ginger cake (on the previous page), I've decided to go for a traditional Parkin – similar to a gingerbread but a heavier cake made with oatmeal, as oats were the staple grain of the Pennines from which this cake originates. Versions appear in recipe books across the history of the WI, many from the cake's home in the counties of Yorkshire and Lancashire where every family would have had their own recipes, up to modern versions such as this adapted from Liz Herbert's Women's Institute's Cakes *from 2009. It's best stored for a week to let the wonderful sticky texture and full flavour develop properly before cutting. In Yorkshire they classically serve it with a wedge of cheese such as Wensleydale.*

Makes 12–16 slices · Preparation 30 minutes · Cook 1–1¼ hours

125g golden syrup
125g black treacle
90g butter, cubed
90g dark brown sugar
125g self-raising flour
1 tsp bicarbonate of soda
2 tsp ground ginger
½ tsp ground cinnamon
225g fine oatmeal
1 large free-range egg, beaten
2 tbsp milk

1 Preheat the oven to 150°C/fan oven 140°C/gas mark 2. Butter and line an 18cm deep square cake tin. Put the syrup, treacle, butter and sugar together in a medium heavy-based pan and heat very gently until melted. Cool for 5 minutes.

2 Sift the flour, bicarbonate of soda and spices together into a mixing bowl. Stir in the oatmeal. Make a well in the centre of the dry ingredients, add the egg, milk and pan contents and mix to a smooth batter.

3 Pour into the prepared tin and bake for 1–1¼ hours until firm to touch. Remove from the oven and cool in the tin. The cake will sink slightly in the middle. Wrap in parchment and foil and store for a week to allow the spicy flavour and sticky texture to develop.

'Join the WI for the ability to challenge yourself and really discover what makes you the person you are – a totally empowering experience'.
Little Bowden WI member

Economy Cake

The first decade of Home & Country *magazine was predominantly dedicated to reporting what was happening in institutes around the country; including federation news, and essays on everything from dancing and music, to acting. Remarkably few recipes appeared, and those that did often consisted of little notes under Helpful Handy Hints! (such as the Rabbit Pudding on page 33), alongside tips on household management. This simple recipe appears ahead of a piece on 'Talks on Economics', which advises that 'the housewife studies to know how she can get the best value for the time and money she has to spend. And she contrives and patches and darns and saves'. A version of this cake exists in Canadian recipe books of the time, where it was also known as Poverty Cake, so it may have arrived here via Canada.*

Makes one 1kg loaf · Preparation 20 minutes · Cook 1 hour

100g soft light brown sugar
150g lard
250g stoned raisins (or mixed dried fruit)
1 tsp cider vinegar
1-2 tsp mixed spice
pinch of salt
300g plain flour
½ tsp baking powder
1 tsp bicarbonate of soda

1   Preheat the oven to 180°C/fan oven 160°C/gas mark 4. Put the sugar, lard, raisins, vinegar, mixed spice and salt into a medium pan with 250ml cold water. Bring to the boil and simmer gently for 3 minutes. Leave to stand until cold.

2   Sift the flour with the baking powder and bicarbonate of soda and mix into the cooled sugar and fruit to give a soft consistency. Spoon into a greased 1kg loaf tin and bake for about 1 hour until golden, well risen and firm to touch. Cool on a wire rack and serve sliced and buttered.

W.I. Economy Cake

Eggless, Butterless, Milkless cake

Ingredients: *1 teacup brown sugar, 1 teacup water, 1 teacup lard, 1 teacup stoned raisins, 1 teaspoonful vinegar, 1 teaspoonful mixed spice, a pinch of salt.*

Method: *Boil in a saucepan for three minutes, let stand until cold, then add 2 teacups flour, ½ teaspoonful baking powder, 1 teaspoonful carbonate of soda dissolved in warm water. Well mix, put in a greased tin, bake for about one hour.*

Home & Country
1921

Rabbit Pie

Regular recipe suggestions for rabbit appeared in the pages of Home & Country. *In times of shortage, rabbit was a precious source of meat, skins and even wool. Early issues of the magazine carried advice on cooking, skinning and curing rabbit, with detailed descriptions of the easiest way to dispatch your 'snared or tame rabbit' and a tip for curing the skin ('to make the skin glossy... rub in shampoo powder... brush it out with a velvet pad'), sitting alongside simple recipes such as this steamed savoury pudding.*

Eating rabbit makes as much sense today as it did a hundred years ago. Wild rabbits are plentiful, free range and the meat is lean, with a mild gamey flavour. We've updated the recipe and cooked it with a suet pastry crust, but it is also excellent steamed.

Serves 4–6 · Preparation 1 hour 15 minutes · Cook 30 minutes

1 tbsp olive or sunflower oil

2 rabbits, jointed (ask your game dealer or butcher to do this) or 1.2 kg diced rabbit

175g piece smoked streaky bacon, rind removed and diced

1 large onion, finely chopped

1 large carrot, diced

2 tbsp each chopped flat-leaved parsley and thyme

about 300ml dry cider (or water)

15g butter

1 tbsp plain flour

salt and freshly ground black pepper

For the pastry:

225g self-raising flour

100g suet

cold water, to mix

beaten egg, to glaze

1   Heat the oil in a large frying pan and add the rabbit joints with the bacon dice. Brown well on all sides then transfer to a large pan. Add the onion, carrot and herbs to the rabbit and season. Pour in the cider or water to just cover, bring to simmering point and skim off any bits of scum. Cover and leave to simmer gently for about an hour or until the meat comes off the bone easily.

2   Meanwhile, make the pastry. Mix together the flour and suet with plenty of seasoning in a bowl. Add 3–4 tbsp cold water and mix with the blade of a knife to form a soft dough that leaves the bowl cleanly.

3   Remove the rabbit pieces and pull the meat off the bone with your fingers. Place in a pie dish with the bacon and vegetables.

4   Simmer the stock from the rabbit until reduced to about 500ml. Mash the butter with the flour to a smooth paste, then whisk into the stock in the saucepan in little pieces. Bring to the boil, whisking, and simmer until thickened. Season and pour over the rabbit.

5   Preheat the oven to 190°C/fan oven 170°C/gas mark 5. Roll out the pastry on a lightly floured work surface until 2.5cm wider than the top of the pie dish. Cut a 2.5cm strip from the edge of the pastry and press onto the dampened rim of the dish. Brush with water and cover with the pastry lid, pressing firmly to seal the edges. Pinch to seal or mark with a fork. Make a small hole for steam to escape, brush with beaten egg and bake for 30 minutes or until golden brown.

Helpful Handy Hints!
Rabbit pudding

Home & Country
1921

*One rabbit, a few slices of bacon or ham, pepper and salt, suet paste.
Cut the rabbit into neat pieces, line a pudding basin with suet crust. Lay
in the pieces of rabbit with the bacon intermixed, season to taste, and
pour in cupful of water; cover with the crust over the top, press it down
with the thumb and finger, and boil for two hours. Boned rabbit is good.*

Christmas Pudding

The work involved in preparing a plum pudding in the early 1920s had recently become easier. Refined white flour and baking powder were well established and now suet could be bought ready shredded. An advertisement in Home & Country *promises the new product 'Makes good cooking easier', compared to the laborious process of buying suet – beef or mutton – from the butcher in a lump, then chopping or grating it at home. Sugar was also available ground to a powder rather than in loaf form, and the country was in the process of moving over to the production of its own sugar from farmed sugar beet. Mrs Beeton's* Family Cookery *carried five different Christmas pudding recipes amongst her pages – including 'rich', 'inexpensive' and 'fruitarian' – made without suet but with butter, sweet almonds, pine kernels and Brazil nuts.*

The updated recipe is based on one that appeared in the WI's Complete Christmas *and is very similar to the original.*

Makes 1 pudding serving 8–12, or 2 smaller puddings serving 4–6
Preparation 25 minutes, plus standing overnight · Cook 4–6 hours

125g ready-to-eat prunes,
   chopped
225g each raisins, currants
   and sultanas
50g mixed candied peel
grated zest and juice of 1 lemon
1 medium apple and carrot,
   grated
225g dark brown muscovado
   sugar
225g shredded suet (you can
   use vegetarian)
100g fresh white breadcrumbs
125g plain flour
1 tsp mixed spice
½ tsp each ground cinnamon,
   coriander and nutmeg
3 large free-range eggs, beaten
150ml dark ale or milk
1 tbsp black treacle

1 Place the dried fruit and peel in a large mixing bowl and add the lemon rind and juice and grated apple and carrot. Mix together the sugar, suet, breadcrumbs, flour and spices and add to the bowl. Mix everything thoroughly. Whisk the eggs with the ale and the treacle and add to the bowl. Mix well with a large wooden spoon. Cover the basin with a tea-towel or cling film and leave to stand overnight.

2 The next day spoon the mixture into one buttered and base-lined 1.5 litre pudding basin or two 600ml basins. Level the surface and cover the basin(s) with baking parchment and foil with a pleat in the centre to allow for expansion. Tie securely with string and make a string handle to lift the pudding with.

3 Steam in a steamer for 4–6 hours, topping up with boiling water as necessary. Remove the pudding and leave to cool. Recover with fresh parchment and foil and store in a cool dark place for at least a month and up to six months.

4 On Christmas Day re-steam the pudding for a further 2 hours. (You can also reheat it in a microwave but remove the foil. The resulting pudding will not be as dark in colour.) Turn onto a warm serving plate, and flame with rum. Add a sprig of holly and serve.

Plum Pudding

Ingredients: ¼ lb. bread crumbs, ½ lb flour, ½ lb suet, ½ lb sugar, ½ lb currants, ½ lb Valencia raisins, ¼ lb orange peel, 1 lemon, 1 salt-spoonful of salt, 1 apple or carrot, 2 eggs, ½ pint milk, 2 teaspoonfuls mixed spice, ½ teaspoonful nutmeg, ½ teaspoonful baking powder

Method: For Xmas pudding the currants ought to be washed and the raisins stoned, and the orange peel cut up in pieces; grate the lemon rind and squeeze out the juice; if an apple is used it must be peeled and chopped and if a carrot, the red part of it grated. Put in a basin all the dry ingredients, including the apple, lemon rind and juice, and mix them all together. Beat the eggs well, add them to the milk and pour among the ingredients in the basin, mixing thoroughly. Butter a pudding basin or mould, and pour the pudding in; cover with a piece of buttered paper, and steam for four hours. Serve hot with either custard or sweet melted butter sauce.

'Like the WI, I want to take on challenging areas, not merely comfortable ones.' **Rt Hon John Bercow MP, Speaker of the House of Commons**

Shortbread

1923 found the WI getting into its stride as a movement with nearly a decade under its belt. In January of that year there were 2,932 WIs, up from 140 in 1917, and membership stood at 174,929. In the December issue, Home & Country was full of news of Christmas pageants, plus correspondence that sheds light on the ongoing debate about an 'institute song'. A significant letter penned by WI member Grace E Hadow, reports attending 'Exhibitions or Council meetings at which the whole assembly has joined in singing Blake's Jerusalem'. The writer urges other WIs to write in to headquarters to ask that this practice to be approved nationally. Jerusalem was sung at the AGM for the first time the following year.

This shortbread recipe appeared in the December issue, and many versions turn up throughout WI publications and in households across the UK - with every cook declaring that their own is the very best. The updated recipe is a typical example of one of the countless variations.

Makes 14 fingers · Preparation 15 minutes · Cook 12–15 minutes

200g plain flour
100g butter, cubed
50g caster sugar

1 Sift the flour into a bowl. Stir in the sugar and rub the butter in until the whole mixture comes together. Press the mixture into a 17–18cm square tin.

2 Preheat the oven to 160°C/fan oven 140°C/gas mark 6. Bake the shortbread for 12–15 minutes or until pale golden. Cut into fingers.

Home & Country
1923

Shortbread

Ingredients: *1 lb. butter, ¾ lb. flour, ¾ lb. sugar.*

Method: *Mix sugar and flour, break up butter and mix in with a knife. Put mixture in tins, smooth with knife and prick all over with a fork. Bake in slow oven.*

WI market stall in Saffron Walden,
1930s

1926–1935

Education, education, education

In its earliest days, the aims of the WI included encouraging countrywomen to become involved in growing and preserving food to feed the war-torn nation. A decade later, this had developed into a commitment to educate and to encourage women to become active citizens. The world was changing rapidly, especially after the end of the war, with shifts to the social order as people moved away from traditional roles in service. There were new methods of food production, imported ingredients and new labour-saving devices for the home.

Preparing and cooking good nutritious food for her family and managing the household budget were seen as essential skills for the modern housewife, and the WI responded accordingly. Lady Denman chaired a government committee to look at 'practical education of women for rural life', and the annual resolution of 1927 called for the establishment of 'short courses in Domestic Science to include food values and household budgeting'.

Independent from external funding for the first time and with the new National Federation of Women's Institute headquarters opened at 39 Eccleston Street in London in 1926, the movement could really start to develop its remit to improve the quality of life in the rural community. Shortly after, in 1928 women finally gained the same voting rights as men and could vote from age 21. In 1931, and facing a severe economic crisis, the government turned to the NFWI (made up of almost 300,000 members by 1930), to look at improving cooking and nutrition skills. WI markets were set up across the country and a grant was given to set up a full-scale co-operative business, with the aim of selling surplus produce – increasingly important as the Great Depression took its toll on the country.

Helping members and their families eat well in times of hardship was a large part of the remit for *Home & Country* through this challenging decade. In February 1926, a new series was launched in its pages. Mrs Margaret MacFarlane would spend the next three months outlining, in considerable detail, the steps the house wife of the time should take to ensure her family was properly fed. Her advice was specific: 'it is essential to realise that the body demands a well-balanced diet, and that the quality of the food, i.e. its nutritive value, is as important as its quantity'. And, having set out her views on 'food value and general economy', she continues: 'People do not easily get tired of a well-cooked dish, but still if a particular dish is served too often it will outstay its welcome'. Her words still ring true today!

First NFWI Chair,
Lady Denman, 1925

Oatmeal Porridge

Mrs MacFarlane's weekly menu for feeding a family served up porridge every morning bar Sunday. Porridge has seen a huge resurgence in popularity nowadays, as the importance of breakfast as part of a healthy diet is restated by health experts. Oats, with their high protein, slow-release energy, cholesterol-lowering fibre and vitamin content (vital folic acid and vitamin B1) have been hailed as a trendy 'super food'.

At home, soaking oats overnight in the water results in a morning bowlful that is velvety smooth, and aficionados think it well worth the effort. Aga owners can bring their porridge to the boil, cover and place in the warming oven of the Aga overnight. The next morning, stir and bring back to simmering point, adding more water if necessary.

Serves 3–4 · Preparation 5 minutes · Cook 20–30 minutes

100g pinhead oatmeal
pinch of salt (optional)

1 Bring 800ml water (or a mix of water and milk if you must) to the boil in a medium pan. Pour in the oatmeal in a continuous stream, stirring as you go. Cook over a low heat for 20–30 minutes, stirring regularly with a wooden spoon. Serve with cold milk or single cream and light brown sugar or warmed honey and fresh or dried fruit.

**Home & Country
1926**

Porridge

Stir in four good handfuls of oatmeal to a quart of boiling water and stir constantly for ten minutes until it begins to thicken. Then add a tablespoonful of salt, and leave to simmer for half an hour or longer if possible. Stir it occasionally, as it is liable to singe, and serve in bowls with cold milk.

Fried Bread

Beat an egg in half a pint of milk and brush this thoroughly over five slices of bread. Then fry in bacon fat until a golden brown, drain and serve. Bacon can be cooked with the bread if liked.

Scotch Broth

As her menus attest, Mrs MacFarlane was obviously a Scot pining for the dishes of her homeland. As well as classic porridge, she included Stoved Potatoes (see page 26), and this Scotch Broth and Dumplings in her weekly menu planner. Our updated version is wonderful cooked in a slow cooker or overnight in an Aga. The flavour improves with keeping. If you like dumplings, add them 30 minutes before you are ready to serve the soup.

Serves 4–6 · Preparation 15–20 minutes · Cook 2 hours

1 medium onion, chopped
1 large turnip, diced
1 small carrot, diced
1 large leek, sliced
1 small parsnip, diced
100g pearl barley
1 litre lamb or mutton stock
   (or cold water)
175g shredded leftover lamb
   or mutton
50g kale, shredded (optional)
salt and freshly ground
   black pepper

1 Place the prepared vegetables in a large pan with the barley and stock or cold water. Season and bring to the boil, then simmer at the lowest heat for 1½–2 hours until the barley is tender. Add more water if the broth gets too dry.

2 Stir in the leftover meat and kale (if using) and continue cooking for 10–12 minutes. Check the seasoning; it needs plenty of pepper. Serve in warm bowls.

3 If you want to add dumplings, follow the original recipe but use 85g shredded suet stirred into 125g self-raising flour, with plenty of seasoning and enough water to make a stiff paste. Add chopped fresh parsley and thyme if desired. Drop into the top of the broth and cook for the last half hour.

*Home & Country
1926*

Scotch Broth and Dumplings

3 quarts cold water, 1 marrow bone, 1 turnip, 1 carrot, 3 leeks, small parsnips, cauliflower, etc., two dessertspoons pearl barley. Put the barley and the bone in the cold water. Cut the vegetables into dice, and add together with the seasoning, when the stock has been boiling for an hour. Continue boiling gently, skim well and serve.

***Dumplings**. Rub 6 ozs shredded suet into ½ lb flour, add 1 teaspoonful of baking powder, seasoning and enough water to make a stiff paste. Form into small balls, flour, and drop them into the soup an hour before the time to serve. If liked a piece of beef or mutton can be substituted for the bone, and it can be cut up or served with the meat, or separately.*

Fish Cakes

Mrs MacFarlane's menus suggest fish cakes for a Saturday breakfast. Simple fish cakes are a great family meal and a thrifty way to use up leftovers if you've cooked too much fish. This recipe starts from scratch but can be made with flaked cooked fish and cooked mashed potato. I sometimes add chopped capers or even mashed leftover peas and some finely chopped mint for variety.

Serves 4 · Preparation 25 minutes · Cook 15 minutes

300g old potatoes, peeled and
   cut into small cubes
20g butter
300g smoked haddock, cod
   or salmon fillet
100ml milk
juice of ½ lemon
chopped parsley and chives
   (optional)
2–3 tbsp plain flour
freshly grated nutmeg
1 tbsp olive oil
salt and freshly ground
   black pepper

1 Cook the potatoes in plenty of boiling water for 15–18 minutes until tender, then drain thoroughly, return to the pan, and dry quickly over a low heat. Mash with half the butter and seasoning. Transfer to a large mixing bowl and leave to cool.

2 While the potatoes are cooking place the fish in a shallow pan and add the milk to just cover – top up with water if necessary. Bring to the boil and poach gently for 8–10 minutes until just cooked through – the flesh will be opaque. Drain off the liquid and flake the flesh. Stir gently into the potato with the lemon juice and herbs (if using). Check seasoning.

3 Shape the mixture into eight patties (or 16 mini ones). Place the flour in a shallow bowl with nutmeg and seasoning and dip the fishcakes in it to coat lightly. Chill until needed.

4 Heat the olive oil with the remaining butter in a shallow non-stick frying pan and fry the fishcakes on both sides for 6–8 minutes until golden, turning once. Drain on kitchen paper and serve with tomato ketchup.

Fish Cakes

To half a pound of cold flaked white fish add half a pound of mashed potatoes, seasoning and a gill of milk. Mix thoroughly and form into small round cakes. Flour these and fry in shallow fat until a golden brown.

Home & Country
1926

Steamed Sponge Pudding

Around 150 recipes were collected from members of Wiltshire's WIs to feature in 'Secrets of Some Wiltshire Housewives' (1927). As editor Edith Olivier says in her foreword, 'most of them are in constant use, and many have been handed down in one family for some generations'. These local books and leaflets, many stored in regional archives of the federations, provide 'a treasury of wisdom' that reveals much about our culinary heritage, so easily lost, with recipes handed down across generations.

Versions of a steamed sponge pudding such as this one have appeared regularly in WI recipe books. As Jane Grigson wrote in her introduction to the Puddings chapter in English Food *(1974), "English puddings have always had a great reputation since the seventeenth century –perhaps earlier – and they deserve it'. She suggests serving her steamed ginger pudding, similar to this, with a luxurious sauce rather like a zabaglione. She also advocates a thin egg custard, which works well here.*

Serves 4–6 · Preparation 15 minutes · Cook 1½ hours

100g butter
100g caster sugar
2 large free-range eggs, beaten
225g self-raising flour, sifted
50ml milk
3 tbsp jam or golden syrup

1   Butter a 750ml pudding basin. Cream the butter with the sugar until pale and fluffy. Beat in the eggs a little at a time. Fold in the flour with the milk to give a soft dropping mixture.

2   Spoon the jam or syrup into the bottom of the basin, and add the creamed mixture on top, spreading it level. Cover with greaseproof paper and foil with a pleat in the middle to allow for expansion. Tie in place with string and steam over simmering water for 1½ hours.

3   To serve, remove the covering, place a warm serving plate over the basin and invert. Leave for a few minutes for the jam or syrup to run down the side then remove the basin. Serve with extra warmed jam or syrup and custard or pouring cream.

Secrets of Some Wiltshire Housewives 1927

A Dozen Puddings from One Recipe

The foundation recipe is for plain sponge pudding.

Rub 2½ ozs. margarine into 6 ozs. of flour, add a pinch of salt, a heaped teaspoonful of baking powder, and 3 ozs sugar. Beat an egg; mix it with half a cupful of new milk, and stir it into the other ingredients. Pour into a well-greased basin and steam for 2 hours. Serve with a jam or fruit puree sauce.

This admits of the following variations when the sauce served would be custard or cream:-

(2) After greasing basin, pour 3 tablespoonfuls of raspberry jam in the base and pour the plain mixture over.
(3) Ornament the basin with large stoned raisins before using the plain mixture.
(4) Add the handful of currants and raisins or a half quantity of each to the dry ingredients.
(5) Add 2 ozs. of well-washed and chopped figs.
(6) Add 2 ozs. chopped dates weighed after stoning.
(7) Add the rind and juice of a lemon to the flour, etc. and use a little less milk.
(8) The same as above, but orange instead of lemon.
(9) Mix a tablespoonful of cocoa with the flour, and two extra tablespoonfuls of milk.
(10) Before adding egg and milk to dry ingredients, stir in 3 tablespoonfuls of strawberry jam.
(11) Mix 2 ozs. dessicated cocoanut with flour, etc.
(12) Flavour with strong black coffee or with coffee essence, and before putting mixture into basin put in some halved shelled walnuts.
Mrs. Smith, Codford.

'Borough Belles WI is a fab way to learn about the local community, meet like-minded women, be inspired and indulge in yummy cake!' **Borough Belles WI member**

Chicken Mousse with Fresh Peas and Tarragon

In the summer of 1930, journalist H Pearl Adam was a fresh voice writing for Home & Country. *Her cheery tongue-in-cheek advice on catering is all about having fun and relaxing with the family. Here she is on the subject of tennis supper dishes: 'Not even the servant problem can excuse the monotony of the usual tennis supper. O far too often cold meat and salad, it's time to give the poor old lettuce a rest.' Instead she suggests this chicken recipe, managing to have a sly dig at Wall Street bankers and their wealth in the process...*

We've updated it to a mousse, a lovely summer starter or light lunch when fresh peas are in season.

Serves 4–6 as a starter · Preparation 15 minutes

100g fresh or frozen peas
225g cooked chicken breasts
juice and rind of 1 small lemon
1 tbsp chopped fresh tarragon
3 tbsp mayonnaise
1 tsp Dijon mustard
3 tbsp whipped double cream
salt and freshly ground black
   pepper
red and white chicory leaves,
   to serve

1 Cook the peas in boiling water for 2–3 minutes until tender. Drain and refresh under cold running water to keep the bright colour. When cold, pat dry with kitchen paper.

2 Remove any skin from the chicken and discard. Cut the meat into small pieces and place in a food processor with the lemon rind and juice, tarragon, mayonnaise and mustard. Process to form a smooth mousse. Add the peas and pulse to mix into the mousse but don't overwork. Fold in the whipped cream. Season to taste. Chill until needed.

3 To serve, place spoonfuls of the mousse on to the stalk ends of the chicory leaves. Arrange on a serving platter and scatter with chopped chives.

Home & Country
1930

Wall Street Chicken
If somebody gives you some money, follow the recipe for meat below but with chicken and green peas slowly stewed and moistened with their own water. Leave the peas whole and mask the turned out mould with the rest of the water boiled to half its bulk, thickened with ground rice, and, if Wall Street has been really good, richened with cream.

Meat Loaf Creamed
Bring raw meat cut into small lumps to a state of tenderness by dropping them in boiling water and stewing them so slowly that one can just hear the water slowly bubbling in the closed pot. Keep the water for jelly or soup. Put the meat through the mincer or pound it with left over vegetables or potato puree; mix it with a beaten egg to the half pound: moisten it to a thick paste with milk, cream or broth. Pour it into a buttered mould lined with breadcrumbs and give it half an hour in a moderate oven. Turn out when cold, and slice.

Raspberry and Banana Trifle (or Not)

H Pearl Adam rounds off her tennis supper menu with a dish that supposedly takes her reader away from the ubiquitous trifle. But not that far, it would seem, as her alternative, with its layers of sponge, jam, custard and cream, still manages to resemble her nemesis. It's a dish, however, that can sit happily in a cold place, allowing her family to finish their tennis game, 'that last set is the best of all, as everybody knows, especially when the last balls are exchanged in the gentle nine o'clock dusk.'

The 1920s saw the first domestic fridges become widely available to the public. Mrs Beeton in the 1927 edition Family Cookery *considers a 'refrigerator, though not a necessity, is invaluable for preserving such perishables as milk and butter'. Few countrywomen would have had fridges or expected to have one, as most villages had no electricity supply and would still not have until well beyond the end of the next war. A north-facing larder with a cold slab, made of stone or marble, was the norm.*

Serves 6–8 · Preparation 20 minutes, plus chilling

1 packet trifle sponges
 (4 sponges)
3–4 tbsp raspberry jam
 (homemade is best!)
2–3 ripe bananas, sliced
200g fresh raspberries
50g desiccated coconut
150ml fresh orange juice
4–5 tablespoons brandy
 or sherry
500g carton ready-made
 custard
300ml double or whipping
 cream
extra fresh raspberries and
 toasted flaked almonds to
 decorate

1 Split the 4 sponges in half horizontally and sandwich them together with the raspberry jam. Cut into cubes and arrange in the bases of 6–8 glass serving bowls. Scatter the bananas and raspberries over the top of each bowl of sponge. Sprinkle with the coconut. Mix together the orange juice and brandy or sherry and pour over the fruit to soak into the sponge.

2 Spread the custard over the fruit and level the surface. Whip the cream until just holding a peak then pile onto the custard to cover. Decorate with raspberries and toasted flaked almonds or even chopped chocolate – despite what Mrs Adam says about the flavour, I think it works. Chill for several hours to let the flavours combine. (Or follow Mrs Adam's recipe and keep layering up the ingredients as she suggests. Either way it's a wonderful summer dessert...)

Getting away from Trifle

And from fruit salad! Put a layer of sponge-biscuit crumbs, very finely crushed, in the bottom of a glass dish, then a layer of jam, then a sprinkling of desiccated coconut, then one of crushed banana, then one of whipped cream then custard. Continue until the dish is full. Pour a little milk over it as though it came from a watering-pot. Leave it in a cold place for at least two hours. Then cover it with cream crushed up with crumbs. I have had it with chocolate on the top and it looked delicious, but the chocolate was not right with the other flavours. A dash of lemon juice with the jam is excellent. Of course, if there are crushed strawberries or raspberries instead of jam....! If possible let them be crushed beforehand and lie in the orange juice before you use them.

Home & Country
1930

Apple and Rosemary Jelly

The September 1930 issue of Home & Country *sets out the aims of the WI: 'The main purpose of Women's Institutes is to improve and develop... rural life by providing centres of educational activities and social intercourse.' This theme is followed through with practical recipes using apples – including this jelly – details of a paper pattern for a 'really becoming frock', an advertisement from a reader selling 'Two good song records', and tips on thrift.*

Makes 9 x 225ml jars · Preparation 1 hour, plus straining overnight

3 unwaxed lemons
1.5kg Cox's Orange Pippins
   or cooking apples, washed
   and coarsely chopped
4 bushy sprigs fresh rosemary
   (you can also use sage or
   thyme)
granulated sugar (see recipe)

1 Pare the rind from one of the lemons and cut into fat shreds. Squeeze the juice. Place in a heavy-based pan with the apples and rosemary and just enough water to cover. Bring to the boil and simmer for 30 minutes or until the apples are soft. Spoon into a jelly bag or muslin-lined sieve suspended over a large bowl and leave to drip overnight. Do not squeeze the bag or the jelly will be cloudy.

2 The next day measure the liquid and pour it into a preserving pan with 450g sugar per 600ml. Stir over a low heat until the sugar has dissolved. Bring to the boil and cook rapidly until a set is reached (see page 86).

3 Remove the pan from the heat, skim off any scum, cool for a few minutes then pour into hot sterilised jars. Seal with waxed discs and lids and leave to cool completely. Label and store in a cool, dark place.

Home & Country
1930

Great Grandmother's Pippin Jelly

Great grandmother's jelly was sparkling, clear and not too sweet, with a delicate flavour of lemon. She always used the same old recipe and no-one ever had a better. She would take sound pippins and pare, core and quarter them, to every twelve allowing one quart of water and a little thinly cut lemon rind. She would set them on the fire and when they had boiled to as [sic] mash, let the liquor run twice through a jelly bag, till it ran bright and clear. Having first measured the juice, she would boil it just ten minutes, when to each pound she would put ¾ lb sugar. After the sugar had dissolved she would boil it fast. She never had jelly that would not 'jell' and fast boiling was the secret. She would keep it skimmed, and the children would hold the saucers the while. They liked preserving time! As soon as a few drops set on a plate it was done. Into each jar she would put a little shredded candied peel, first washed and dried. The jelly would be almost set before the pots were filled. No sooner than was this done than she would make the pulp into apple marmalade, using half its weight in sugar.
C.J. Robertson M.C.A.

Apple Amber

The silhouette of Windsor Castle graces the cover of the first edition of the Berkshire Federation's recipe book, From Hand to Mouth – Cookery Recipes and Household Hints, where you'll find this recipe for Apple Amber, a baked tart topped with meringue. This substantial publication carried a preface from Lord Ernle, where he writes tellingly: 'Too many cooks, of course, spoil the broth, but the more the merrier in framing recipes.'

Serves 4–6 · Preparation 30 minutes · Cook 1 hour

300g shortcrust pastry,
   homemade or shop bought
25g butter or margarine
500g Bramley apples, peeled,
   cored and sliced
75g demerara sugar
grated rind and juice of 1 lemon
2 large free-range eggs,
   separated
25g caster sugar, plus extra for
   dredging

1 Preheat the oven to 180°C/fan oven 160°C/gas mark 4. Roll out the pastry and use to line a shallow 23cm pie-dish or pie plate. Bake blind for 20 minutes then remove the baking beans and return to the oven for a further 5 minutes until the pastry is almost cooked.

2 Meanwhile, melt the butter or margarine in a medium pan, add the apples, sugar and lemon rind and cook gently over a low heat for 20–25 minutes until soft. Push through a sieve. Beat the egg yolks into the apple purée with the lemon juice and spoon into the pie dish. Spread level. Bake for 20 minutes or until the pastry is cooked and the apples just set.

3 Whisk the egg whites until stiff then whisk in the caster sugar and continue to whisk for a minute. Pile the meringue onto the pudding, making sure all the apple is covered and there are no gaps. Dredge with caster sugar and return to the oven for 10–15 minutes until the meringue is crisp and golden. Serve hot or cold with pouring cream.

Hand to Mouth
1932

Apple Amber

Ingredients: *1 lb. apples (peeled), 3 oz. of Demerara sugar, 1 lemon, 2 oz. of margarine, 2 eggs, Pastry*

Method: *Line a shallow pie-dish with short pastry rolled out thin. Melt the margarine, add the apples and cook a little, then add the sugar and lemon rind very thinly peeled. When quite soft rub fruit through a sieve. Beat up the yolks of eggs and add to the puree, also the juice of the lemon, and put in the pie-dish. Place in a moderate oven and bake for 20 minutes or until the pastry is cooked and the apples just set. Whip the whites of the eggs to a stiff froth and add a little castor sugar. Pile this on the pudding, dredge castor sugar over and brown lightly in a cool oven. Serve hot or cold.*

Strawberry Short Cake

In 1932 the ladies of Berkshire WI may well have had American members, as two recipes appear in the pages of their cookery book, From Hand to Mouth, *that use US-style cup measures. Maybe an American heiress had married into English aristocracy, or travelled 'across the pond' on one of the number of newly built luxury ocean liners that regularly made the crossing.*

Strawberry Short Cake made with 'soda biscuits', or what we might recognise here as scones, has many references in American recipe books of the mid-1800s, when parties were held to celebrate the strawberry season. Maybe one of the Berkshire WI members attended one and brought the recipe home. Our updated recipe makes eight individual short cakes or one large one. The cakes freeze well so can be made in advance and reheated gently. We've left out buttering the warm short cakes but you can do so if you like.

Serves 8 · Preparation 15 minutes · Cook 12–15 minutes

325g plain flour, plus extra
    for dusting
3 tsp baking powder
large pinch of salt
100g chilled unsalted butter,
    diced
3 tbsp caster sugar
1 large free-range egg
125ml full-fat milk

For the filling:
300g fresh strawberries, hulled
1–2 tbsp caster sugar
250ml double cream, whipped

1 Preheat the oven to 220°C/fan oven 200°C/gas mark 7. Sift the flour, baking powder and salt into a mixing bowl. Rub the butter into the dry ingredients until they resemble coarse breadcrumbs. Stir in the sugar. Whisk the egg with the milk, and pour into the flour mixture a little at a time, using a flat-bladed knife to mix. Bring together to form a soft dough.

2 Turn the dough out onto a lightly floured work surface and roll out gently to a thickness of about 2cm. Lightly flour a 6cm round cutter, and cut out as many rounds as you can. Reroll the scraps and cut out more rounds so that you have eight in total. Place well apart on a greased baking sheet and brush the tops with milk. Bake for 12–15 minutes until golden brown. Leave to cool for 5 minutes on a wire rack.

3 While the short cakes are cooking, crush half the strawberries with the sugar, and slice the remaining strawberries, depending on their size. Split the warm short cakes and top one half with a spoonful of the crushed strawberry mixture and a few sliced strawberries. Spread the top half with whipped cream. Replace the top and serve.

Strawberry short cakes

*2 cupfuls of flour, 4 teaspoonfuls of baking powder, ½ teaspoonful of salt,
2 teaspoonfuls of sugar, ¾ cupful of milk, ¼ cupful of butter*

*Mix the dry ingredients, sift twice, and work in the butter with the tips of the fingers,
and add milk gradually. Toss on a floured board. Divide in two parts. Roll out each half
until it will fit into a round layer cake tin. Bake about 12 minutes in a hot oven. Split
while hot, and spread with butter. Crush strawberries, sweeten to taste, warm slightly;
put them between split short cake and on top. Serve hot with cream. If desired, extra
strawberries, crushed and sweetened, may be passed with the cream.*

This will make two short cakes; if only one is desired, divide the recipe in half.

Toad in the Hole

Writing in the preface to her local federation's Cornish Recipes, Ancient and Modern, *first published in April 1929, Edith Martin of Tregavethan, Truro, says 'The Recipes have been printed exactly as received, and if... there is some slight repetition... it is because it varies in different districts, each of which claims theirs is the right one'. There are in fact five separate recipes for Toad in the Hole and only the first, shown here, bears any resemblance to the version still familiar to us today. Another is simply pieces of steak folded into pastry, yet another a suet and potato cake with pieces of ham tucked into it.*

Look online nowadays and you will find Toad in the Hole recipes from every 'celebrity chef' from Delia to Jamie, Nigella to Nigel Slater. But the idea of cooking meat in a 'hole' can be traced right back to Hannah Glasse, who cooked pigeon that way in The Art of Cookery *(1747).*

Serves 4 · Preparation 15 minutes · Cook 30–35 minutes

300ml full-fat milk
3 medium free-range eggs
1 tsp vinegar (optional)
100g plain flour
1 tsp baking powder
1 tsp English mustard powder
30g lard or dripping
6–8 good sausages
salt and freshly ground black
   pepper

1   Preheat the oven to 220°C/fan oven 200°C/gas mark 7. Pour the milk into a bowl and whisk in the eggs with the vinegar (if using) and plenty of seasoning. As the original recipe says, 'hand-shake in the flour', baking powder and mustard powder very lightly, whisking all the time to make a batter. Leave to stand for 15 minutes.

2   Heat the fat in a heavy-based roasting tin (about 32 x 26 cm) on top of the stove. Add the sausages and brown on all sides over a high heat. Pour the batter over the top and bake for 30–35 minutes until golden brown and well risen. Serve immediately.

Toad in the Hole

Ingredients: 2 breakfast cups of flour, 1 teaspoonful baking powder, 1 teaspoonful vinegar, 1 pint milk, 3 eggs, 1 lb. sausages

Method: Pour the milk into a bowl and well whisk in 3 eggs with a pinch of salt and the vinegar; then hand-shake in the flour and baking powder very lightly, beating all the time. Pour into a well-greased flat baking tin and arrange sausages on top of the batter. Well pricked steak could be used instead of sausages if preferred. Time, 1½ hours in a nice oven.

Shortlanesend W.I.

'I congratulate the NFWI on the work it has undertaken in talking to vulnerable women, who have made it clear that the Bill will leave them without support or access to protection under civil remedies.'
Baroness Gould, House of Lords on the LAPSO Bill

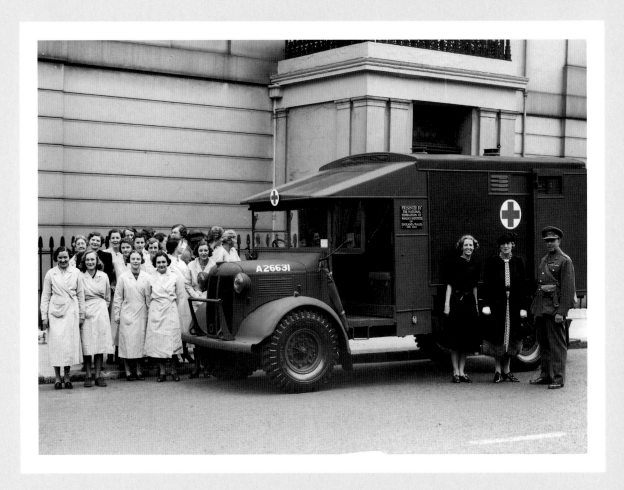

Ambulance presented to the Army by the NFWI London,
1941

1936–1945

Keeping the nation together

'Without doubt we Women's Institute members are a remarkable race' – so wrote the editor of *Home & Country* in her 'News from the Counties' report on the early stages of the war in November 1939. And, she continued, 'there is nothing whatever Institutes are not doing in this war', from leading the Land Army, as Chair Lady Denman was, 'down to sharing a saucepan with a lonely London mother, like Mrs Jones down the lane'.

Lady Denman's own message emphasised that 'every one of us can help keep alive a spirit of steadiness and freedom from panic'. She spoke of 'our small share in winning the victory which we believe will come'. And though she might not have known it at the time she was writing, the women of Britain were indeed to play a vital part in keeping the nation together through the dark days of the war.

Make do and mend was the order of the day, and the members of the WI were skilled at the art. Everything and anything that could be reused, was: from clothing

repaired repeatedly and then cut down for children, to aluminium pots and pans, melted down and used for aircraft parts. Paper was in short supply – witnessed by the fact we now have few of the many pamphlets and information booklets produced during the period, as waste paper was collected door to door by the 'rag and bone man'. Envelopes were used over and over again and many federations no longer have records from the time as they gave up the paper they were written on to support the war effort.

By 1945 the full impact of the activities of the country's women in support of the war effort were receiving more recognition. 'The high degree of mobilization achieved in this war has been largely due to the contribution made by women' was announced in a White Paper on the War Effort. By working in industry, civil defence work and in 'part time service, paid or unpaid, in connection with the war effort', in addition to 'their domestic duties', hundreds of thousands of women had 'released men and younger women for the services', and by the last years of the war, allotments, largely managed by women, had increased in numbers from 800,000 at the outset to more than 1½ million.

Left image
Wartime fruit preservation
centre, 1940

Right image
WI members at work at the School for
Produce Guild members, 1940s

Vegetable Salad

Despite the looming prospect of war, spring 1939 saw Home & Country *still preoccupied with more everyday matters. In a feature on Picnic Fare in the May issue, readers were advised that, 'Food to be eaten outdoors should both pack easily and be easily handled when unpacked'. A savoury turnover fits the bill, as 'it cuts down all unnecessary fuss' and they could also take along a vegetable salad (recipe below). Finally 'a slice of good cake rounds off the picnic lunch admirably!'*

At the start of the war Britain was importing over two thirds of all its food. To preserve stocks, rationing began on January 8, 1940. Initially rationed foods were bacon, butter and sugar. This was soon extended to cover eggs, cheese, cooking fat, milk, jam and tea. Citrus fruit and bananas became scarce too. Bread was not rationed, until between 1946 and 1948, so WI cooks soon became adept at bulking out dishes with fillers such as potatoes and breadcrumbs.

Home & Country
1939

Vegetable Salad

So many convenient cartons and cases are now available for packing picnic fare that it is possible to pack either a fresh green salad or a cooked vegetable one without any inconvenience. A simple cooked one, delicious with cold ham, is made by cooking some peas with plenty of fresh mint; drain them and let them go cold; then dress them lightly with a mixture of oil and vinegar, salt and pepper, and pack into a large carton.

COOKING THIS RECIPE TODAY...
Try adding cubed feta cheese and sliced spring onions in an olive oil and lemon dressing.

'We pride ourselves on the fact that our membership is very diverse – we're for everyone.'
Darling Roses WI member

Bean and Lentil Soup

With the outbreak of war, the WI was once again at the forefront of the country's efforts to support and feed its citizens. The editor of Home & Country *encouraged readers to 'do what we can to maintain that spirit of sanity... which has been the mark of WIs since their foundation'. Housing and feeding evacuees, preparing ground for vegetable growing or keeping a few poultry, utilising allotments, and assisting farmers who may be short-handed – all were to be encouraged as ways for members to help.*

Serves 4 · Preparation 15 minutes, plus soaking overnight · Cook 1½ hours

200g dried cannellini or
   haricot beans
1 fresh bay leaf
1 tbsp olive oil or lard
1 large onion, finely chopped
1 stick celery, diced
1 large carrot, diced
1 large potato, diced
1 clove garlic, chopped
1 large sprig fresh rosemary,
   leaves chopped (optional)
200g brown lentils
100g fresh spinach, washed and
   shredded
salt and freshly ground black
   pepper

1   Cover the beans with cold water and soak overnight. The next day, drain them, place in a pan with the bay leaf and cover with cold water. Bring to the boil and simmer for 1 hour till just tender. Drain, reserving the beans and liquid.

2   Heat the oil or lard in a heavy-based pan, add the onion, celery, carrot, potato and garlic and cook over a low heat for 5 minutes until softened. Add the rosemary, if using, the lentils, 800ml cold water and season. Bring to the boil and simmer gently for 15–20 minutes until the lentils are tender.

3   Add half the cooked beans to the pan with the spinach, and cook for a further 3–4 minutes. Purée coarsely with a hand-held blender or mash with a vegetable masher. Add 500ml of the bean cooking liquid and bring to the boil.

4   Stir in the remaining beans for the last 3–4 minutes, adding extra water if necessary. Check seasoning. Spoon into warm serving bowls and serve with extra virgin olive oil for drizzling and grated Parmesan.

*Home & Country
1939*

Nourishing Meals for Young England

Strict economy of food is a national duty... The following suggestions may prove helpful to those with children – both their own and evacuees under their care.

Here is a delicious soup, the nutritive value of which is increased by the addition of milk. Take a cupful of white beans, a cupful of lentils, one carrot, one potato, a teaspoonful of tapioca for each person, a handful of spinach, two quarts of water, one ounce of dripping, salt, pepper and vinegar. Soak the beans and lentils overnight; then drain. Put the water, salt and pepper in a pan and when boiling add the beans, lentils, sliced carrot, potato and tapioca, and cook until tender. Wash and dry the spinach, cook it in a little dripping until the latter is absorbed then add to the soup. Rub the ingredients through a sieve or colander. Reheat, add more seasoning if needed, a little vinegar and a little hot milk. Serve with bread.

Quick Fresh Raspberry 'Jam'

In the second week of the war the NFWI heard that fruit across the country was going to waste due to the lack of sugar. So members sprang into action and 'made representations to the authorities'. Four hundred and thirty tons of sugar was sent out to members and The Produce Guild was formed with a grant of £500, with the aim of helping in the vital production and preservation of food. Advice on preserving valuable fruit without sugar had appeared in H&C a month ahead of the sugar for jam initiative. But it was not an ideal method, as can be seen from the rather worrying notes of caution. By the following year, home canning was being encouraged instead as a way to preserve extra produce as a vital part of the war effort, and 500 Dixie 'hand sealers' (canning machines) were provided to WIs for the purpose, sent specially from America.

Nowadays, we aim to consume less sugar in our diets generally, so we've included a modern quick-cooked fresh 'jam', which can be made successfully with less sugar.

Makes two 350g jars · Preparation 15 minutes

500g fresh raspberries, washed
150g granulated sugar
juice of ½ lemon

1   Place the raspberries in a pan with the granulated sugar and heat gently until the sugar dissolves. Simmer for 8–10 minutes until thick and syrupy. Pour into warm sterilised jars and cover. Leave to cool then label and store in the fridge. Use within a month. The jam will have a softer set: use it to sandwich cakes or on scones with whipped cream.

Home & Country
1939

From the Editor's desk

The first few weeks of the war threw the Institutes into some bewilderment... with halls commandeered, many officers absorbed in other activities, and travel facilities so reduced that movement seemed... impossible, Institutes... began to ask themselves whether they had better not close for the duration. Fortunately this... soon passed. The whole spirit of the movement, which was born in times of difficulty, is opposed to despondency.

Preserving Apples Without Sugar

Wash the apples well, remove stalk and discoloured parts, do not peel. Cut in sections, place in a pan with 1 pint water to 4 lbs apples (less water if apples are juicy and soft). Stir with a wooden spoon until the juice flows freely. Cook gently until quite soft. Sieve and return pulp to pan to reheat. Bring to the boil. **THIS IS IMPORTANT.**
Have the bottles very hot, fill one at a time, put on the rubber ring cap, and clip or screw band, and seal at once.

If no vacuum bottles are available... pour over an inch layer of warm (not hot) mutton fat. Do not move the bottle... until quite set. The whole success of the process depends on putting on the fat... while the pulp is still very hot... The pulp should be kept boiling the whole time... and the bottles kept hot.

Plums and blackberries can be pulped in this way. No water need be added after washing if the fruit is ripe... Damsons may require a little water. Pulped fruit is best put up in small quantities as it does not keep long when once the bottle is opened. It can be used for puddings of various kinds, tarts, sauces, fools and chutneys, and can be made into jam, when sugar is available, using ¾ lb of sugar to 1 lb. pulp.

'We wanted to encourage diversity in the WI and learn more about 'traditional' skills. We also believe in campaigning.' **Gothic Valley WI member**

Stuffed Cod with New Potatoes

'Waste nothing' was the motto for the 'home food controller'. Stock made from vegetable parings, bacon rinds and bones; vinegar and bicarbonate of soda to raise puddings and cakes, and save valuable eggs, and advice on using sour milk in scones and breads, were all recommended ways to make precious food supplies go as far as possible.

Fish was plentiful, inexpensive and nutritious – and not rationed – but in a feature in Home & Country *on making the most of fish, the reader was reminded that 'both its economy and nourishing properties depend largely on the manner in which it is cooked'.*

Serves 4–6 · Preparation 15 minutes · Cook 1 hour

750g new potatoes, thickly
    sliced
1 bunch spring onions, cut into
    short lengths
3 tbsp olive oil
750g piece cod fillet, skin on
100g fresh white breadcrumbs
2 tbsp chopped flat-leaved
    parsley
3 tbsp chopped fresh tarragon
1 tsp capers, finely chopped
grated rind of ½ lemon
½ tsp freshly grated nutmeg
1 large free-range egg, beaten
salt and freshly ground black
    pepper

1 Preheat the oven to 220°C/ fan oven 200°C/gas mark 7. Arrange the sliced potatoes and onions over the base of a deep roasting tin and season. Sprinkle with two tablespoons of the oil and seasoning and toss together to coat. Bake for 15 minutes until starting to brown.

2 Meanwhile rinse the cod under cold water and pat dry with kitchen paper. Cut into two equal pieces. Mix together the breadcrumbs, herbs, capers, lemon rind, nutmeg and seasoning. Beat the egg with the remaining tablespoon of oil and add to the breadcrumbs to bind. Pat the mixture over the surface of one piece of cod (on the opposite side to the skin). Arrange the other piece of cod on top to cover. Slash the skin on each piece a couple of times, then tie neatly into a parcel with string. Brush with oil.

3 Remove the potatoes from the oven and stir to loosen. Lay the cod on top and cook for 15 minutes in the hot oven then turn down the oven to 180°C/fan oven 160°C/gas mark 4 and cook for a further 20–25 minutes until the fish is cooked through and the flesh flakes easily. Remove the string and serve in slices with the potatoes and a green vegetable.

Stuffed Cod Steak

Have a thick slice of cod – about one and a half pounds in weight – and have it cut through the middle lengthwise, but without separating the pieces. For the stuffing rub one and a half ounces of either dripping or margarine into a teacupful of breadcrumbs; add two teaspoonfuls of chopped parsley, a little salt and pepper and a dust of grated nutmeg. Use a little milk to bind these ingredients and press this stuffing in between the slices of fish. Put into a pie dish or casserole, put some pats of dripping on top, and over all sprinkle a teacupful of oatmeal that has been toasted for a few minutes in the oven. Pour a little water around the fish and bake in a moderate oven for about an hour.

Mincemeat Slice

As Christmas approached in 1940 not everyone was feeling very festive. In many families there were empty places round the table: many children were far from home as evacuees, men – and some women – were at the front. But despite rationing, Home & Country *magazine urged readers to spare precious ingredients and pack up a parcel to send to the forces. A Mincemeat Roll was deemed to be easier to make than individual pies – and easier to post. The updated recipe is based on Star Mince Pies in the* WI Complete Christmas *book. Buy the best mincemeat you can find and stir in extra brandy. You can also make this with ready-made puff or shortcrust pastry. Choose one made with butter for the best flavour.*

Serves 6–8 · Preparation 30 minutes, plus chilling · Cook 25–30 minutes

225g plain flour
100g butter, diced
50g lard, diced (or use all
    butter)
25g icing sugar
1 large free-range egg,
    lightly beaten
450g good-quality mincemeat,
    ideally homemade
100g fresh cranberries (optional)
egg white and caster sugar,
    to finish

1 For the pastry, sift the flour into a mixing bowl and rub in the butter and lard until the mixture resembles coarse breadcrumbs. Stir in the icing sugar. Beat the egg with a tablespoon of iced water and add to the dry ingredients. Bring together to form a stiff dough, knead lightly then wrap and chill for half an hour.

2 Preheat the oven to 190°C/fan oven 170°C/gas mark 5. Roll out the pastry to an oblong about 30cm x 45cm. Cut in half down the centre to create two thin lengths. Place one half on a damp baking sheet and spread with the mincemeat, leaving a border of 2.5cm around the edge. You can scatter over fresh cranberries here to add colour and flavour. Fold the other rectangle in half lengthwise (long sides together) and make cuts at an angle 5cm apart, leaving a 5cm border. Open out and use to cover the mincemeat. Press the edges together to seal and pinch with finger and thumb to create a decorative edge. Chill for 15 minutes.

3 Brush the roll with whisked egg white and scatter with caster sugar. Bake for 25–30 minutes until the pastry is golden and cooked through. Slice and serve warm with brandy butter.

Christmas Fare for Absent Friends

As Christmas draws near our thoughts go to absent friends and relatives – men and women on duty, children and others forced from home by war conditions – who, this year, will be unable to spend with us what is the great English family festival of the year. But we can send them an expression of our thoughts in a parcel of good things. Let your choice fall on dainties that will pack easily and carry well. Eggs are scarce but we can get a few, and would willingly sacrifice them to give those far away pleasure. Pack your parcels strongly, and post them in good time, putting the address inside the parcel as well as on the outer cover.

Mincemeat Roll

Time and trouble is saved and good carriage assured by making a large mincemeat roll instead of a quantity of small pies. Roll the pastry into a strip and spread it with mincemeat, roll up and secure the edges and bake in a moderate oven.

'*Meet like-minded people, have fun, link with the community, get inspired to learn new and interesting things.*' **Wardy Hill WI member**

Apple and Fig Roll

To add to the challenges a nation at war was facing, the winter of 1939-40 was the most severe for 45 years. Fuel and food were in short supply and ingenuity was essential for women trying to keep families warm and fed. Dried fruit and vegetables contributed good flavour and variety – both frequent watchwords for WI members when planning meals.

Serves 6 · Preparation 30 minutes, plus soaking overnight · Cook 1½ hours

50g dried apples, soaked in
  warm water overnight
50g dried figs, soaked in
  warm water overnight
grated zest and juice
  of 1 orange
300g plain flour
1 tsp baking powder
100g shredded suet
grated nutmeg
2 tbsp golden syrup

1 Put the fruit with the soaking water in a saucepan with the orange rind, and simmer very gently for 5 minutes until tender. Drain well, reserving the cooking water, and cut the fruit into small pieces.

2 Preheat the oven to 180°C/fan oven 160°C/gas mark 4. Sift the flour with the baking powder, stir in the suet and bind to a soft dough with a little of the water in which the fruit was cooked. Roll it out to an oblong shape about 1 cm thick. Arrange the fruit in layers over the pastry, sprinkle with grated nutmeg and golden syrup.

3 Moisten the pastry edges with water, roll up and fasten securely, wrap in foil and place on a greased baking sheet. Bake for 1–1½ hours until puffed and golden. (You can also wrap it in a clean tea towel and steam it.) Unwrap carefully and transfer to a warmed serving plate. Serve with plenty of custard.

Home & Country
1940

Even in normal times spring is expensive on account of the scarcity of fresh fruit and vegetables, and this year, after an unusually severe winter, difficulties are considerably increased. But there is good nourishment and flavour in dried fruit and vegetables – indeed these might have an advantage over early products, which never have the fully developed flavour possessed by varieties that have been preserved in their prime.

Home & Country
1939

Apple and Fig Roll

Have 2 oz. each of dried apples rings and dried figs washed and soaked in warm water for 24 hours. Put them, with the soaking water, into a pan with orange and lemon rind, and cook gently until tender. Drain them – saving their soaking water – and cut the fruit into small pieces. Make a piece of pastry with three-quarters of a pound of flour, 4 oz. dripping, half a teaspoonful of baking powder and use the water in which the fruit soaked for mixing. Roll it out in oblong shape, about one-third of an inch thick. Layer the fruit on the pastry, sprinkle with grated nutmeg and trickle over a little golden syrup. Moisten the edges of the pastry, roll up, fasten and bake in a moderate oven. The remainder of the soaking water may help to make a sweet sauce for serving with the roll.

Boiled Chocolate Cake

Cakes, which used precious eggs and sugar, became a rare treat in wartime, baked only for special occasions. Substitute ingredients were recommended. In 'Good Things for Tea – with Less Fat and Sugar', a feature in the January 1940 issue of Home & Country, *mashed potatoes appeared in recipes for rock cakes, jam buns and parkin, while other recipes used oatmeal to make bread and scones.*

I found this recipe, a family favourite that belonged to my grandmother, written in a wartime notebook, and current WI member Daphne Thompson remembers it being made for special occasions by her mother. Margarine allowance was 4oz a week, sugar 8oz a week, while the ration of one fresh egg a week and a packet of dried once a month, demonstrates why bakers of the period had to show imagination and versatility. Milk was also rationed – household milk given in the original recipe was dried milk as opposed to fresh.

Makes 1 loaf cake · Preparation 15 minutes · Cook 50 minutes–1 hour

1 tbsp instant coffee, made up
   with 200ml boiling water
75g butter or margarine
75g dark muscovado sugar
1 tbsp golden syrup
225g plain flour
25g cocoa
1 tsp bicarbonate of soda
100g dark chocolate chips
3 tbsp milk
½ tsp vanilla extract

1 Preheat the oven to 180°C/fan oven 160°C/gas mark 4. Butter and base-line a 500g loaf tin. Put the coffee, butter or margarine, sugar and syrup into a pan and heat slowly to boiling point. Boil for 5 minutes then leave to cool.

2 Sift the flour, cocoa and bicarbonate of soda into a mixing bowl and add the boiled ingredients and the chocolate chips, milk and vanilla extract. Spoon the mixture into the prepared tin. Cook for 20 minutes then reduce the heat to 170°C/fan oven 150°C/gas mark 3 and cook for a further 30 minutes until the cake has risen and a skewer emerges cleanly from the centre.

3 Cool in the tin slightly before turning out onto a wire rack.

Chocolate Boiled Cake

Member's recipe 1941

Put one tea cupful of black coffee (Camp), 3 oz. of margarine, 3 oz. sugar and dessertspoon of golden syrup into a pan and heat slowly to boiling point. Boil for 5 mins then leave to cool. Add ½ lb. flour and 1 tablespoon of cocoa, sifted together, then 1 teaspoonful bicarbonate of soda dissolved in 2 ½ tbsp of milk and lastly add ½ teaspoon of vanilla essence. Put mixture in floured tin (1lb size) and bake about 1 hour in a moderate oven, reducing the heat after 20 mins Regulo 3, 350F, reduced to Regulo 2, 325 C. When cooked, cool in the tin slightly before turning out. When quite cold, cut through the centre and spread with the following mixture: 1 good tablespoon golden syrup, 1 level tablespoon cocoa, 1 level tablespoon household milk, then the top can be iced and decorated as liked.

Lamb Pot Roast

Saving energy was as important as making food go as far as possible and avoiding waste during the war. Conditions in the average country cottage were primitive; an outside privy, oil lamps and a pump for water in the kitchen. Cooking was mainly done on a range but fuel was at a premium so planning food that cooked with the minimum use of energy was important – pot roasts were ideal. In December 1944 the house coal quota was cut. A letter to Home & Country *wondered 'how best we countrywomen can deal with the knotty problem of cooking, washing and warming our rooms during the winter, with an allowance of 4 or 5 cwt. (112lb or 50kg) in January and we don't know what in February... We shall deal with it, of course, we always do.'*

Serves 6–8 · Preparation 15 minutes · Cook 2–2½ hours

1.5kg boneless shoulder
   joint, rolled
2 tbsp olive oil
2 cloves garlic, sliced
2 sprigs fresh thyme
300ml stout or meat stock
salt and freshly ground
   black pepper

1 Preheat the oven to 170°C/fan oven 150°C/gas mark 3. Season the lamb shoulder. Heat the oil in a flameproof casserole and brown the lamb on all sides. Add the garlic and thyme to the pan and pour in the stout. Cover the pan and cook in the oven for 2–2½ hours until the lamb is tender and cooked through.

2 Remove the lid for the last 30 minutes for the meat to brown. Once the lamb is cooked, remove from the pan and leave to rest for 10 minutes. Simmer the lamb juices to reduce by half. Strain into a warmed gravy boat and keep warm. Serve with the nettle champ on page 152, made with curly kale if the early nettles are past.

Pot Roasting

Pot Roasting is very similar to oven roasting but the job is done on top of the stove in a very heavy pot instead of the oven. In effect the pot is turned into a miniature oven.

To Pot Roast any joint or bird: *First calculate the cooking time as you would for oven roasting – but allow five minutes per pound longer. Choose the heaviest pot you have, which must have a lid. See that the joint or bird just fits into it nicely. It doesn't matter if you have to squeeze it in – the joint will shrink slightly in cooking.*

Melt some fat in the pot, enough to cover the bottom to a depth of, say, half an inch. Heat this fat to the 'blue haze' stage and put in your joint or bird. It will sizzle violently. Keep the heat fairly high and turn the joint over until it is nicely browned on all surfaces. Now reduce the heat until, with the lid on the pan, you can hear a steady sizzle. Leave it like this until the cooking time is up, but turn the joint occasionally so that it is cooked fairly evenly all over.

The amount of heat necessary to keep the joint sizzling is surprisingly small. The saving in fuel cost, as compared to oven roasting, is considerable. And it means a cooler kitchen.

You can cook potatoes round the joint in the pot but they will not be crisp as oven roast potatoes are, but they taste very nice just the same. Another thing you can do is to add some chopped carrots and onions to the hot fat before you put the joint in. This seems to improve the flavour of the joint, and the vegetables blend into the fat to form a rich, dark, gooey liquid, which is delicious.

'The WI gives people a forum for joining others to do something they would perhaps not do on their own.'
Sylvia Beardshaw, WI member

Chicken Pie

Even before the war, a chicken was a luxury for most people, and one to be enjoyed only occasionally. Birds were killed for the pot once they stopped laying so were likely to be tough old fowl that needed long slow cooking. The wartime cook was rarely able to put chicken on the menu. Philip Harben, who was arguably our first celebrity chef, was a regular contributor to Home & Country *with his 'In the Kitchen' page: here he shares his ingenious method for making the most of a chicken.*

Serves 6 · Preparation 20 minutes · Cook 1¾ hours

1 good quality free-range
   chicken, about 1.5 kg
stock vegetables (a carrot,
   onion, celery stick, leek all cut
   into chunks)
a bay leaf, 6 peppercorns, sprig
   or two of fresh thyme
50g butter
1 medium onion, chopped
50g plain flour
50ml single cream or full-fat
   milk
3 tbsp chopped flat-leaved
   parsley
100g smoked ham, shredded
350g puff or shortcrust pastry
   made with butter
beaten egg, to glaze
salt and freshly ground black
   pepper

1   Place the chicken in a large pan to fit snugly with the stock vegetables. Pour over enough cold water to almost cover and a large pinch of salt. Bring to the boil and then cover and simmer very gently for 45–50 minutes until the juices run clear when the thickest part of the leg is pierced with a skewer. Cool in the stock for a really good moist finish. Strain the stock and measure out 600ml.

2   Preheat the oven to 200°C/fan oven 180°C/gas mark 6. Melt the butter in a large non-stick pan and add the onion. Cook gently for 3–4 minutes until soft and pale. Add the flour and stir for a minute to cook. Off the heat gradually whisk in the hot stock then return to the heat and simmer, stirring until thick and smooth. Stir in the cream, parsley and seasoning.

3   Remove the chicken meat from the bones, discarding the skin. Tear into pieces and mix with the ham in the base of a 2-litre ovenproof dish or roasting tin with a wide lip to hold the pastry. Pour over the sauce (you can make the pie to this stage then cool and chill overnight). Place an eggcup or funnel in the centre to support the pastry. Roll out the pastry on a lightly floured work surface to a rectangle 5cm larger than the dish. Cut a strip of pastry about 1.5cm wide and place along the edge of the pie dish.

4   Brush the pastry edge on the dish with cold water then lift the pastry over and settle it gently over the filling. Pinch around the edges to seal and make a hole in the centre to allow steam to escape. Chill for 15 minutes to allow the pastry to rest then brush with beaten egg and bake for 45–50 minutes until crisp and golden. Serve.

One way of making a chicken go a long way would be to serve everybody with a tiny portion of bird and a lot of (say) potatoes. But that is to evade the problem – potatoes do not taste like chicken. We can give everyone their share of chicken and at the same time provide a dish which is as nourishing as it is tasty, as substantial as it is delicious. The recipe makes use of, indeed it actually requires for the best results, the rather fat American bacon which the grocer (he can't help it) wishes on us from time to time. I am going to pre-suppose that you have a fowl weighing some four to five pounds, and I will keep all the other ingredients in proportion. This will make a pie sufficient for at least ten people.

Home & Country
1945

Chicken Pie

Having plucked and drawn the fowl, remove all the meat from the bones. Break up all the bones, including the carcase, put them in a pan with carrots, onion, bay-leaf etc., cover with water and simmer for an hour or two. The amount of stock yielded should be just about a quart. If there is more, boil it rapidly and so reduce it. Herein lies the secret, all the flavour from the bones must be concentrated in that quart of stock. Cut up the chicken meat and giblets and cook them in the stock at just below simmering point for at least half an hour. Meanwhile cut up a quarter of a pound or more of streaky bacon into small pieces and fry it in a couple of tablespoons of margarine until the bacon has become crisp and yielded its fat. To this fat add four tablespoons (4 oz) flour, stir to make a roux. Add slowly the chicken pieces in their stock, stirring and cooking until it thickens.

Now you have your chicken and bacon in a thick creamy sauce, all of it tasting well of chicken; in fact all of the nourishment of the bird and every particle of its luxury taste is concentrated in the mixture. If you add a cup of dried household milk powder to the roux before the liquid goes in, you will improve and enrich the dish still further. Another valuable addition is a handful of coarsely chopped parsley.

Now make a short or flaky paste. Use grated cheese, if you can. Put the chicken and sauce into a pie dish, cover with the paste, brush with reconstituted dried egg and bake. I have seen 200 hungry men sprint to a canteen when this dish was on the menu.

'The WI really is what you make of it. There are so many opportunities and events – there really is something for everyone.'
Whiteley WAGs WI member

Gingerbread Animals

The whole time-consuming and tedious process of ensuring no glimmer of light was to be seen during the blackout, not even the glow of a cigarette, had a far-reaching effect on everyday life. Holding regular WI meetings was a challenge. But the importance of giving people the chance to 'let their hair down' was also recognised. One of Lady Denman's earliest instructions at the outbreak of hostilities was 'to keep the social side of the WI alive... to laugh together will send us home heartened and cheered for our daily work'.

The blackout lasted until April 30, 1945 and for Londoners it was the illumination of Big Ben that symbolised the ending of more than five years of darkness.

Makes 18 · Preparation 10 minutes · Cook 15–20 minutes

50g golden syrup
100g butter or margarine
225g plain flour, plus extra
  for dusting
½ tsp bicarbonate of soda
1 tsp mixed spice
2 tsp ground ginger
50g caster sugar
1 medium free-range egg yolk
beaten egg, currants or pieces
  of dried fruit

1 Preheat the oven to 180°C/fan oven 160°C/gas mark 4. Put the syrup in a pan with the butter and heat gently to melt. Sift the flour with the bicarbonate of soda and spices. Stir in the sugar. Add the melted ingredients with the egg yolk, mixing well until you have a stiff dough.

2 Roll out on a floured work surface and cut out as animal biscuits using cutters, or follow instructions below for making a cat, using beaten egg to stick pieces together. Bake on greased baking sheets for 15–20 minutes until pale golden. Cool on sheets for 5 minutes then transfer to a wire rack.

Home & Country
1945

With the lifting of the black-out, this winter there will be more coming and going in the villages during the evenings about Christmas time. Here are some suggestions for snack foods and an economical hot punch drink that carollers might appreciate.

Home & Country
1945

Gingerbread Animals

2 oz. golden syrup or sugar, 2 oz. margarine, 8 oz. plain flour, ½ level teaspoon mixed spice, 2 level teaspoons ginger, lemon substitute to taste, 1 level teaspoon soda bicarbonate, a little dried egg, reconstituted, a few currants or pieces of dried fruit.

Melt in a pan syrup or sugar with margarine. Pour into bowl. Add some flour, the spice and lemon substitute. Stir well. Dissolve soda bicarbonate in a tablespoonful of tepid water and add to the mixture. Continue stirring and gradually add more flour. Finish by turning out the mixture onto a floured board and knead in the remainder of the flour. For a cat, roll out a small round for head, a larger round for body, flatten these and roll a strip for the tail. Join with a little reconstituted egg and put currants or pieces of dried fruit for eyes. Bake in a moderate oven for 5–10 minutes according to size.

Women Demand Equal Pay campaign action,
1950s

1946–1955

Rebuilding the country

The January 1946 issue of *Home & Country* magazine opens with congratulations to Willey WI, Shropshire, 'for being the 6,000th Institute formed... a proud distinction'. During that year the number of WIs would increase by around 30 a month and, by its close, membership stood at 303,000. But WI members, new and old, had a struggle on their hands. On the same page as the announcement of the latest WI, there was also an appeal from the Queen to those members of the Women's Land Army about to be demobilised after six years of work, 'to carry on the constructive work... and understanding of the life and problems of the country, with the need to give its dwellers as good opportunities as the town dwellers'.

The coming year would be one of 'rehabilitation and reconstruction' and, as had been the case during the war years, the women of the WI would continue to play a vital role in rebuilding the country post war. Austerity Britain faced problems with the food supply, housing shortages, and the challenge of rebuilding families torn apart by war. WI members were urged in an editorial 'to turn our faces forward to the problems of peace'. Two of the biggest issues facing the countryside were only too familiar to WI members, those of housing and sanitation. A WI survey from 3,500 institutes, published in 1944, revealed that just under a third of rural parishes still had no piped water supplies; half were without sewerage, while fewer than 10% of agricultural workers' homes had electricity.

Rationing, of food, fuel and other everyday essentials would continue for most of the next decade. The importance of educating women in 'household economy' was an ongoing WI priority. In 1948 the WI's own college for the education of women was finally launched in Oxfordshire, after much preparation. At its formal opening,

Hyde Heath WI Litter Pick campaign action, 1954

educationist Sir Richard Livingstone said: 'Education's purpose is to assist us... to do the things we want to do and cannot do without help'. Denman College (now known simply as Denman) was there to help women 'widen horizons and let light into one's mind'. And it continues to do so to this day.

Top image
Essex WI market stall, 1950s

Bottom image
Hand sealing preserve machine

Scotch Pancakes (Girdle Scones)

As the world moved rapidly on in the post-war reconstruction period, a nostalgia for pre-war times and customs was revealed in WI recipe books and in Home & Country *magazine. Diana, Countess of Albemarle, who succeeded Lady Denman as Chair of the NFWI in 1946, writes in the foreword to* Traditional Fare of England and Wales *(1948), 'At the present time such recipes are in danger of being lost owing to the passing of many country houses as centres of family life'. Numerous recipes for pan-cooked scones exist across the British Isles and some were included in* Traditional Fare. *As the book's editor, Mrs J M Wittington, points out: 'It is misleading... to attach place-names to recipes; for owing to the migration of populations in times of depression, the same methods recur in different parts of the country.' But just to be contrary, we are calling our updated recipe Scotch Pancakes.*

Makes 16 · Preparation 5 minutes · Cook 10–15 minutes

225g plain flour
½ tsp cream of tartar
½ tsp bicarbonate of soda
1 tbsp caster sugar
1 large free-range egg
about 100ml buttermilk or milk
butter or oil, for frying

1 Sift the flour, cream of tartar and bicarbonate of soda into a bowl. Stir in the sugar. Make a well in the centre, drop in the egg, add a little buttermilk or milk and beat well together with a wooden spoon. Continue to add more liquid to make a thick batter.

2 Heat a griddle pan or frying pan with a small knob of butter or oil, and drop on spoonfuls of mixture. When bubbles rise to the surface turn the pancakes with a palette knife and brown them on the other side. Keep warm while you cook the rest. Serve with butter and jam.

*Home & Country
1946*

Pan cakes:

2 teacups plain flour, 2 teaspoons sugar, ¼ teaspoon salt, ¾ teaspoon cream of tartar, 1 teaspoon syrup, 1 egg, milk or buttermilk to mix.

Method: *Sieve the dry ingredients into a basin, make a well in the centre, drop in the egg and syrup, add a little milk, beat well together with a metal spoon, add milk to make the mixture into a thick batter, just thick enough to drop from a spoon. Have girdle or hot plate hot, grease, and drop on spoonful of mixture. When surface rises in bubbles turn with a knife and brown on the other side.*

Corned Beef Hash

The British were introduced to corned beef, a wartime standby, via imports from the US. Although canned food had been a British Army staple since the end of the 19th century, it made its biggest domestic impact in the post-war period. After its suspension during the war, The Canned Foods Advisory Bureau reopened to 'interest housewives in the wider uses of canned food', which was promoted as being both convenient and aspirational. In Home & Country in the early 1950s, a writer wondered if 'it was really true that people nowadays prefer tinned fruit when they can get it fresh?' She had been in a busy restaurant and, on asking about the pineapple dessert, was assured by the proprietor that 'Oh no, madam. I wouldn't serve fresh pineapple. Tinned is so much nicer.' Ministry of Food bulletins and leaflets focused on promoting simple but effective ways to feed families on limited resources and included this Corned Beef Fry (or Hash) recipe – it's still a favourite fast family supper.

Serves 4 · Preparation 15 minutes · Cook 30 minutes

750g cooked old potatoes, cut into 2cm cubes
1 large red onion, finely chopped
340g can corned beef, cubed
4 tbsp chopped flat-leaved parsley
1–2 tbsp chilli sauce (optional)
2 tbsp olive oil
salt and freshly ground black pepper

1   Mix the cubed potato, onion, corned beef, parsley, chilli sauce (if using) and seasoning together in a mixing bowl. Heat the oil in a large non-stick frying pan, add the corned beef mixture and cook, stirring, over a medium heat until the mixture starts to brown and the potatoes crisp up.

2   Preheat the grill. Pat the hash mixture into a flat cake shape in the pan, turn up the heat to brown the base for a couple of minutes. Place the pan under the grill for 3–4 minutes to brown the top. Serve in wedges with a fried egg on top.

Quick cooking for busy days

Corned Beef Fry

Busy Spring-cleaning days call for dishes that are easy to prepare. A large thick frying pan... no fat or less than for ordinary fried dishes... and you don't have to stand over the pan. All recipes are kitchen tested. Issued by the Ministry of Food.

4 oz. diced corned beef, 1 lb mixed cooked vegetables, diced, 1 lb cooked mashed potato, seasoning, ½ oz cooking fat.

Mix together the beef, vegetables and potatoes and season well. Melt the fat and in a pan and spoon in the mixture. Fry for about 10 minutes turning on all sides; finally, allow to brown.

Home & Country 1947

Elderberry and Apple Jelly

The July issue of Home & Country *was dedicated to the establishing of a vital winter store cupboard, with the encouragement to 'Preserve for Plenty'. Every item for the store was to be grown or produced from home, and 'the contents... would be enough for one person for six months (apart from the ordinary rations and green vegetables). Any extra produce was to go to fill the National Store Cupboard: the aim was that every person who was able to, should produce an extra 10 lb of produce to help feed the nation through the coming months. Eighty-five thousand WI members rose to the challenge, and the success of Operation Produce was celebrated with a special exhibition in London.*

Elderberries have low pectin so that's why both the original and updated recipes add apples to ensure a set. Using elderberries in a jelly means there is no need to destalk them as in the original – a fiddly process! They make a wonderful dark but clear jelly – delicious on scones or toast.

Makes about 1kg (3-4 225g jars) . Preparation 15 minutes . Cooking 1¼–1½ hours, plus straining overnight

1kg elderberries, washed
1kg cooking apples (or crab apples), washed and roughly chopped
granulated sugar

1 Place the elderberries in a pan with enough water to just cover. Warm gently to draw the juices then simmer gently for about an hour until tender. Cook the apples in another pan, with just enough water to cover and simmer gently for an hour until quite soft. Combine the two fruit with their juices.

2 Spoon the fruit into a jelly bag or muslin-lined sieve suspended over a large bowl and leave overnight or for at least 12 hours.

3 Measure the juice and put in a preserving pan. Add 300g sugar for each 500ml juice. Heat gently, stir until the sugar is dissolved, then boil rapidly for about 10 minutes or longer, until setting point is reached.

4 Off the heat use a slotted spoon to remove any scum. Pour into sterilised pots, and cover. When cold, label and store in a dark cook place.

Elderberry and apple jam

Blackberries, elderberries, rosehips and other wild fruits make delicious jams, jellies, puddings and pies to add variety and zest to your meals. They're yours for the picking; but do remind the children to be careful to shut gates, to avoid treading on growing crops and to be careful not to break hedges or bushes.

3 lb. elderberries, 3 lb. sour apples or crab apples, 5 lb. sugar

Wash and stalk the elderberries with a fork. Warm gently to draw the juices then boil until tender. Cook apples and simmer in another pan, with just enough water to prevent burning until quite soft. Then pass through a sieve. Add the apples and sugar to the elderberries. Stir until the sugar is dissolved, then boil rapidly until setting point is reached (a little dropped on a cold plate should wrinkle when pushed with the finger).

Sweet Yorkshire Pudding

The WI saw its membership peak during the 1950s. There was nostalgia for times past, as witnessed in this recipe from the 25th edition of the Yorkshire Federation's cookbook Seven Hundred Recipes, *but also the organisation was looking at ways to reflect the changing role of women. Features in* Home & Country *show this tug between the old and the new, covering issues from letters on the theme of 'Just a housewife' – 'for years I've fought and indeed am still fighting to put housework before "hobbies",' wrote Mrs Muriel Chorley, adding 'better a dusty house than a dusty mind' – to articles on the right kind of job for your daughter.*

Modern WI members can identify with this dilemma as we try to balance careers and family life, and once again membership is rising as the support and friendship found in the WI is valued in stressful times.

Our updated recipe for Sweet Yorkshire Pudding will be a familiar dessert to Yorkshire folk, but if you prefer the savoury version just leave out the syrup.

Serves 4 · Preparation 10 minutes, plus 30 minutes standing · Cook 45 minutes

100g plain flour
pinch of salt
2 medium free-range eggs
100ml milk
25g butter
1 tbsp groundnut or
    sunflower oil
warmed golden syrup, to serve

1 Preheat the oven to 220°C/fan oven 200°C/gas mark 7. Sift the flour and salt into a bowl, make a well in the middle and break in the eggs. Mix the milk with 100ml of water. Add a little of the liquid to the 'well' and whisk to make a smooth batter, gradually drawing in the rest of the flour as you go and adding the remaining liquid. Beat for 2 minutes then leave to stand for 30 minutes.

2 Put the butter and oil into a 20–23cm square baking tin and heat in the oven till almost smoking. Pour in the batter and cook for 45 minutes. Pour on warmed syrup and serve at once.

Yorkshire Pudding

Ingredients: 2 eggs, 6 tablespoonfuls of flour, pinch of salt
Put the flour into a basin, make a hole in the middle into which pour a little milk. Break in the two eggs and beat into a smooth batter, and then thin down with a little water.

The joint to be eaten with Yorkshire pudding must be roasted before the fire. Place a shallow baking tin under the joint to catch the dripping. When dripping and tin are quite hot, pour in the batter. When browned on one side, cut into squares and turn. In winter 2 tablespoonfuls of snow can be used instead of eggs. In this case the batter will be slightly whiter.

'All country women are eligible, no matter what their views on religion or politics may be. The movement is strictly non-sectarian and non-political. It is designed to secure the widest possible agreement between the greatest diversity of women.'
1951 *The Times*

Jam Swiss Roll

Food shortages over the previous decade had forced housewives to use all their resourcefulness to create meals to feed their families. While this might have led to a bulldog spirit in the kitchen, a lack of ingredients also created a generation without the opportunity to develop cooking skills that their mothers and grandmothers had taken for granted. Concern about the loss of skills and knowledge was reflected in WI publications aiming to preserve culinary heritage, and in features in Home & Country, *such as this evocative description of how to make the perfect sponge cake. It's worth pointing out that for baking purists, this is a true no-fat sponge, while a sandwich cake is made from a butter-based mix (see page 160).*

For the modern cook, with an electric whisk to hand, a Swiss roll is a lot less work. Our updated recipe is taken from Cakes and Biscuits – Best Kept Secrets of the WI *by Jill Brand. Fill with homemade jam or lemon curd (see page 186) and whipped cream for tea or fold crushed fresh soft fruit into the cream for a dessert.*

Makes 8–12 slices · Preparation 15 minutes · Cook 12–20 minutes

3 medium free-range eggs
75g caster sugar
75g plain flour, sieved
icing sugar or caster sugar,
    for dusting

For the filling:
6 tbsp jam or lemon curd,
    warmed
200ml whipping cream,
    whipped (optional)

1 Preheat the oven to 200°C/fan oven 180°C/gas mark 6. Grease and base-line a 33cm x 23cm Swiss roll tin. Whisk the eggs and sugar together in a deep mixing bowl until the mixture is thick enough to retain a trail left by the whisk. Fold in the flour and spoon into the prepared tin. Bake for 12–20 minutes until golden and springy to touch.

2 Turn out the sponge onto a sheet of baking parchment dusted with caster sugar. Remove the lining paper, trim the sponge edges and spread with warmed jam. Roll up the sponge firmly, using the baking parchment. Dredge with caster sugar and cool on a wire rack.

3 To fill with cream, roll the cooked cake up without jam but with a sheet of fresh greaseproof paper to stop it sticking. Leave to cool completely. Carefully unroll, remove the paper and spread with cream and jam. Re-roll and dust with sugar. Chill until needed.

Perfect Sponge Cake

Sponge cake is a thing about which I am asked more that anything else. It is a cake which many cooks have perforce forgotten how to make. So here is a very safe recipe...the only ingredients are eggs, sugar, flour and patience.

Sponge cake*: the real thing, pre-war standard, nothing barred.*

ingredients*: 3 eggs, 3 oz. caster sugar, 3 oz. plain flour; a little fat (preferably not margarine) for greasing the tin. No baking powder is needed – the eggs do all the raising.*

Spanish Tortilla

As the country slowly started to recover after the war and huge steps in technology gradually filtered down into everyday life, wives could become more adventurous with their cooking. Home & Country was concerned that men who had travelled the world on active service would be bored with the old routines at home 'or fail to appreciate how hard you have been working in their absence'. Women were encouraged to be adventurous in the kitchen – no mean task when there were still shortages – and even to get enough rest to ensure they looked their best. Now that eggs were back in the shops, the cook could look to foreign lands for inspiration such as this Spanish Omelette, showing her husband that she acknowledged his more sophisticated tastes, while showing thrift by using up leftovers.

Serves 4 · Preparation 15 minutes · Cook 25 minutes

2 tbsp olive oil
2 medium cooked potatoes,
    cut into 1.5–2 cm cubes
1 medium red onion, sliced
50g cubed chorizo
1 char-grilled red pepper from
    a jar, sliced (optional)
4 large free-range eggs
salt and freshly ground
    black pepper

1   Heat half the oil in a large frying pan and add the potatoes, onion, and plenty of seasoning. Cook over a medium heat for 5 minutes and until the potatoes are golden. Add the chorizo and red pepper, if using, and cook for a couple of minutes.

2   Put the eggs in a bowl with the seasoning and beat with a fork. Add the hot vegetables from the pan and mix thoroughly. Leave to stand for 5 minutes. Heat the remaining oil in a 20cm non-stick frying pan until very hot and pour in the egg mixture. Stir with a fork, lifting the middle of the tortilla to let the uncooked egg run down into the base. Cook over a medium heat for 4–5 minutes until the egg is set and the base is golden.

3   Place a large plate over the pan and very carefully invert the frying pan to tip the omelette out onto the plate, cooked side upwards. Carefully slide it back in to the pan to cook the other side. To get the traditional cake shape, slide the omelette back into the pan a couple more times until the whole thing is golden brown and cooked through. Turn onto a plate and serve warm or at room temperature.

Spanish Omelette

Ingredients: (for 4 people) 4 eggs, 3 small potatoes (not too floury), 4 peeled tomatoes, fresh or canned, 4 grilled rashers bacon, chopped spring onions, chopped parsley, salt, pepper

Method: Peel, dice, wash and dry the potatoes and fry them in the bacon fat for about 5 minutes. Add the tomatoes, cut up, and fry for a minute. Beat the eggs, add to potato and tomato and the rashers, cut up, salt, pepper, parsley, and spring onions. Heat some bacon fat in an omelette or frying-pan, pour in the mixture and shake the pan with your left hand while you stir the mixture with a fork. Cook for two or three minutes, then turn like a pancake and cook for a minute on the other side. Serve flat.

American Fried Chicken

To those struggling with rebuilding a nation, America seemed a land of plenty relatively untouched by war. GIs posted over here to play a vital role in the invasion, introduced us to a different way of viewing life, and we increasingly looked to this carefree approach portrayed in films and news reports from across the Atlantic. At least we could try some of their recipes – like fried chicken – and see whether any of the glamour rubbed off. Traditionally southern fried chicken is always dipped in milk (some sources say buttermilk) and then flour, never breadcrumbed or battered.

Serves 4 · Preparation 10 minutes · Cook 20–30 minutes

4 chicken pieces, a mix of
   thighs and drumsticks with
   bone in
150ml buttermilk (or plain
   milk)
2 tbsp plain flour
½ tsp each ground ginger
   and smoked paprika
salt and freshly ground
   black pepper
15g butter
2 tbsp olive oil

1 Remove the skin from the chicken – or leave it on if you prefer. Toss the chicken pieces with the buttermilk and leave to marinate for an hour or covered overnight in the fridge.

2 Mix the flour with the salt, pepper and spices. Wipe any excess liquid off the chicken pieces and dip in the flour to coat thoroughly. Heat the butter and oil in a heavy-based frying pan until it is very hot, but not smoking. Add the chicken and brown quickly on both sides. Cover the pan and turn the heat right down to low. Cook for 10–15 more minutes on each side turning once, until golden brown and cooked through. Drain on kitchen paper and serve.

Home & Country
1954

Chicken de Luxe

2 spring chickens, cut in half and flattened, cold milk or water, salt, pepper, ground ginger, flour. For frying: 3 oz. butter, or 1 oz. butter and 2 oz. lard, or 6 tablespoons olive oil For gravy: 2 oz. fat used for frying, 2 flat tablespoons flour and ½ pint either chicken stock, tomato juice, cream or cream and chicken stock mixed.

***Method.** Dip the halved chickens in cold milk or water and drain, but do not wipe them dry. Sprinkle them with salt, pepper and a very little ground ginger and coat with as much flour as will stick to them. Heat whatever fat you are using in a heavy based frying pan until it is very hot, but just not smoking. Add the chicken and brown quickly on both sides. Now add ¼ cup boiling water and cover the pan and turn the heat right down to low. Cook for about 40 minutes. Lift the pieces onto a hot dish and pour over a gravy made by frying 2 tablespoonfuls of flour in the fat in which the chicken cooked and adding any of the liquids given above, together with salt and pepper and stirring until the gravy is cooked.*

Baked Custard Tart

The first Ideal Home Exhibition was held at Olympia in London in 1908. It reopened after the war in 1947, with the launch of the first microwave oven. By the 1950s, the WI was playing its part, contributing ideas and produce for the new Market Place section of the show. It produced a 50-page recipe booklet, County Fare, which was handed out on the WI stand along with leaflets on topics such as Yeast Cookery and Pastry. We've chosen the recipe for pastry for 'flan rings' and our modern version is for a custard tart, adapted from Tarts – Best Kept Secrets of the WI *by Liz Herbert. In 1957 a survey showed the average housewife was spending 75 hours a week on housework, not including the weekends!*

Serves 6–8 · Preparation 30 minutes, plus 1 hour chilling · Cook 35 minutes

For the pastry:
115g plain flour
80g unsalted butter
2 tbsp icing sugar
1 free-range egg yolk

For the filling:
300ml single cream
150ml full-cream milk
½ cinnamon stick, crushed slightly
¼ tsp ground mace
2 large free-range eggs plus 2 large egg yolks, beaten
50g caster sugar
freshly grated nutmeg

1   Place the flour, butter and icing sugar in a processor. Process until the mixture resembles fine breadcrumbs. With the motor running, add the egg yolk and whiz until the mixture just comes together. Turn onto a floured surface and gently bring together with your fingertips. Wrap in cling film and chill for 15 minutes.

2   Preheat the oven to 190°C/fan oven 170°C/gas mark 5. Place a baking sheet in the oven. Roll out the pastry and use to line a 20cm deep loose-bottomed flan tin. Chill for 15 minutes. Bake blind for 15 minutes. Remove the baking beans and paper or foil and bake for a further 5–10 minutes until fully cooked and the pastry is golden. Leave to cool. Reduce the oven temperature to 150°C/fan oven 130°C/gas mark 2.

3   Meanwhile, heat the cream and milk with the cinnamon and mace in a saucepan until just boiling. Whisk the eggs and yolks with the sugar. Strain the hot liquid over the egg mixture, whisking all the time. Strain again into a jug.

4   Pour almost all the custard into the flan case then slide the tart back into the oven and carefully top up with the remaining custard (this will avoid letting the custard spill over the sides of the pastry). Sprinkle with nutmeg. Bake for about 35 minutes until the custard is just set but still wobbly. It will continue to cook in the residual heat once out of the oven. Serve the tart at room temperature.

Pastry leaflet 1954

Pastry 1954

It is said that pastry cooks are born not made; but the art may be acquired by paying careful attention to details and using the correct proportions and methods.

Sloe Gin

Two versions of Sloe Gin are given in the section on liqueurs in the WI's Home-made Wines, Syrups and Cordials, a little book that first appeared in July 1954. It proved so popular that it was reprinted within a year, and stayed in print for the next couple of decades.

In its foreword, civil servant and public relations expert Stephen Tallents pays tribute to the 'pioneer work of the Institutes during these latter years in the recovery and recording of village history... and in the rescue and preservation of neglected and perishable riches... None of them was so ingenious, so daring or so fertile as the happy idea which this book embodies'. The 150 recipes for 'drinks for refreshment on hot days and solace on cold nights' were tested by 'Mr. F.W. Beech of the famous Long Ashton research centre'.

The introduction to the liqueur chapter that contains this recipe reads, 'in view of the present price of brandy, gin, rum and whiskey, these recipes are given mainly for their historic interest'. The author didn't expect anyone to make them but the popularity of the book might suggest readers felt differently.

Makes 1 litre · Preparation 20 minutes, plus 3 months maturing time

Sloe Gin

1 lb. sloes
3 oz. white sugar
1½ pints gin

Stalk and clean the fruit, then prick with a silver fork. Pack the fruit in a Kilner jar, add the sugar and gin and screw down tightly. Store three months in a dark cupboard, inverting the jar occasionally. Strain, bottle and cork.

Home-made Wines, Syrups and Cordials 1954

Following this recipe today...
Use 500g sloes, 75g granulated sugar and 1 litre of gin. Instead of pricking the sloes, the other option is to pick them after the first frost, which softens the skins – or simply freeze the berries before using.

'Men scoffed when the first Women's Institute opened in a summer house in Anglesey. Today the WI are the backbone of rural life, with a membership of nearly half a million, and an influence strong enough to sway governments.' 1953 *The Picture Post*

Shrewsbury Biscuits

With the ending of rationing, WI members made the most of the increased availability of ingredients. Even so, times could still be hard. In Home & Country *at the end of 1954, Vera Cox of the NFWI Marketing sub-committee had plenty of advice for members making food for sale to go 'all out' to tempt their customers in the 'difficult months' following Christmas, when markets often ran at a loss. Keeping things local – like these cakes – was one way to attract customers. What's more, WI members 'can do a lot to keep the old traditional cakes and pies from dying out.' 'A Market near an American Camp could try some American recipes' and what about, she suggests, trying unusual preserves, such as medlar, whortle berry and fig jam, that 'are difficult to get in the shops' and finally, 'a jam mentioned in the West Kent Country Housewives Handbook – High Dumpsie Dearie jam'. As Mrs Cox writes, 'The very name would sell it'.*

Makes around 30 biscuits · Preparation 15 minutes · Cook 15 minutes

100g butter
125g caster sugar
2 egg yolks
175g ground rice
200g plain flour
½ tsp caraway seeds
grated rind of ½ lemon
milk to mix

1 Preheat the oven to 180°C/fan oven 160°C/gas mark 4. Cream the butter with the sugar until pale and light. Beat in the egg yolks one at a time. Add the ground rice, sifted flour, caraway seeds and lemon rind and mix to a stiff dough, adding a little milk if the mixture is too thick.

2 Roll out the dough on a floured surface then cut out biscuits with a 6cm fluted scone cutter, re-rolling the dough as necessary. Arrange on parchment-lined baking sheets and prick the top of the biscuits with a fork to make a pattern. Bake for 12–15 minutes until pale golden at the edges. Cool on the trays for 5 minutes then transfer to wire racks to cool completely.

Shropshire Special Cakes (Eat on All Souls' Day)

Quarter of a pound of ground rice, and quarter of a pound of good white flour and a few carroway [sic] seeds. Beat together a quarter of a pound of butter and a quarter of a pound of well sifted sugar. Add the flour, the ground rice and carroway seeds. Stir in enough well beaten whites of eggs, and then yolks of eggs (probably two of each) to make a paste. Rollout and bake as biscuits.

They should be five inches across.

From a recipe book presented by E. Minton to Aileen King (Radbrook, Shrewsbury)

Shropshire Cookery Book 1955

WI members enjoying tea time at Denman College,
1965

1956–1965

The times they are a-changin'

By the middle of the fifties the country was finally starting to emerge from the years of post-war austerity into a new age of increasing affluence and opportunity. As prime minister Harold MacMillan said in 1957 'Britons have never had it so good'. The economic boom saw a growth in employment with new jobs created for women, and magazines and television advertising promoted all kinds of consumer goods that promised freedom from domestic drudgery. The WI was still moving with the times. United in its aims and work through two world wars and their aftermath, the WI now had to think seriously about how it should represent its members, as women's traditional role in society seemed to be turning on its head.

As part of its new approach Denman ran a course entitled Science and Ordinary People in 1956, for members who were prepared to 'stimulate interest in the subject to their counties'. Lectures covered topics such as the peaceful uses of atomic energy, chemistry and electricity. AGM resolutions of the period were proposed on everything from the dangers of radiation to the provision of facilities for routine smear tests for cervical cancer.

Out in the countryside, however, many long-established WI members were still concerned with more everyday issues, such as the rota for the local fruit and produce show. But even in rural areas the changing role of women and the WI was acknowledged and encapsulated in this statement made by a speaker at a meeting of Cardiganshire members in 1958, who stated that 'the ideal education consists of a balance between Science and the Arts'.

'1915 – Founded in, and for, democracy.' 1963 *The Kent Messenger*

WI delegates at the NFWI AGM, 1965

'What future for the WI?' asked Federation Chair Helen Carey, in her book *Bows of Burning Gold*, on issues facing the WI in the year of 1964. While members were urged not to lose sight of 'spontaneity and freedom essential to volunteer work', they were reminded that 'younger women want discussions on live and controversial issues'.

The pages of *Home & Country* reflect the potentially divisive topics that tested members' thinking during this period. Features on changing eating habits, the Freedom from Hunger campaign, rights for working women, girls' education, the payment of maintenance for divorcees with children, sat alongside advice on caring for new fabrics ('Goodnight in Nylon') and changing skirt lengths and how to wear them. Finally in January 1963, there was news of the Fourth Annual Poultry Feather Hat Festival, part of the National Poultry Show at Olympia – not forgetting plans for celebrating the WI's Golden Jubilee in 1965.

Her Royal Highness the Princess Royal (centre)
and Mrs Harding Frawes (right) attending
produce stall at Golden Jubilee Market, 1965

Royal Pudding

The Norfolk Federation has a history of producing its own recipe books. In its 1957 offering, More Good Recipes, members 'unearthed not only recipes... from the Eastern Counties but also some dating from many centuries back, hidden in the manuscripts of our forebears'. Many are extremely simple, with basic methods. Others reflect local connections, such as Sandringham Jelly and Royal Pudding. Her Majesty The Queen is honorary president and member of Sandringham WI, and pays it a visit every year.

The dessert we've updated may be more familiar to readers as Queen of Puddings, an old-fashioned pleasure to round off a classic Sunday lunch. A special poem from Mrs Dawson of Old Costessey, introduces us to the recipes of the Norfolk WIs.

Serves 4 · Preparation 20 minutes, plus soaking · Cook 45 minutes

600ml milk
15g butter
100g fresh white breadcrumbs
grated rind of ½ lemon
50g caster sugar plus 1 tbsp
2 large free-range eggs,
  separated
3 tbsp apricot or raspberry jam

1 Preheat the oven to 180°C/fan oven 160°C/gas mark 4. Heat the milk in a medium pan to simmering point. Off the heat add the butter, breadcrumbs, lemon rind and 25g of the sugar. Leave to stand for 25 minutes.

2 Beat the yolks into the crumb mixture and put into a buttered 1 litre ovenproof dish. Bake for 25–30 minutes until pale golden and set.

3 Beat the egg whites till stiff and fold in the remaining 25g caster sugar. Cover the pudding with apricot jam and then spoon the meringue on top. Sprinkle with the extra sugar and bake for a further 10–15 minutes until the meringue is golden. Serve with pouring cream.

Norfolk More Good Recipes 1957

Royal Pudding

Ingredients: *3 ozs fine white breadcrumbs, 1 oz margarine, rind of ½ lemon, (grated), 1 or 2 eggs, ½ pint milk, 1 oz sugar, 1 tbsp jam, 2 ozs. castor sugar to each egg used*

Method: *Heat milk to blood heat and pour over crumbs with sugar and lemon rind. Cut margarine into small pieces and stir until melted. Leave to soak for ½ hour. Separate whites from yolks of eggs and stir in beaten yolks. Put in greased dish and bake at Regulo 6 till brown. Beat whites of eggs till stiff, fold in the castor sugar. Cover pudding with apricot jam and then place the beaten white of eggs and sugar on top. Set in slow oven, Regulo ½ for approximately 1 hour. Decorate with glace cherries and angelica.*
Mrs Harvey, Colney, Earlham and District

The Cake of Happiness

I've a recipe here for a wonderful dish,
If you taste it, you'll never regret it;
It isn't of fowl, or flesh, or fish,
But once eat it- you cannot forget it.

It's mixed in the bowl of Experience
And stirred with a spoon of Goodwill;
These are the chief ingredients,
Ground in the Common sense mill.

A pound of belief in Providence,
A pint of Tenderness,
Next a cupful of confidence,
And sweeten with cheerfulness.

Quick Loaf

By 1956 when the much-derided National Loaf was abolished, the country had had its fill of 'dirty grey' bread. Pre-war, white bread had been the preferred choice of all. As Elizabeth David wrote in English Bread and Yeast Cookery, *'for centuries the working man envied the white bread of the privileged' – then in the second half of the 19th century the invention of the roller mill put white bread in the mouths of everyone.*

The WI, vigilant as ever to the needs of the nation's home cooks, recognised that people craved good bread and responded accordingly. In 1957 Home & Country *ran a feature entitled 'Bread without Tears', featuring recipes taken from the WI's popular booklet on Yeast Cookery.*

This updated recipe pays homage to the 'Grant' loaf created by baker Doris Grant during the Second World War to encourage people to eat more bread. It became a classic for home bakers as it was not kneaded and had only one proving. (But our version does need kneading.)

Makes one 500g loaf · Preparation 15 minutes, plus rising · Cook 30–35 minutes

400g wholemeal, granary or
   speciality flour
100g plain flour
1 tsp salt
1 tbsp sugar
7g sachet easy-blend yeast
2 tbsp olive oil

1 Sift the flours and salt into a warm basin. Stir in the sugar and yeast. Mix the olive oil with 300ml hand-hot water and add to the flour. Mix to a soft dough, then turn onto a floured board and knead for 10 minutes until the dough is springy.

2 Shape into a loaf or place in a 500g floured bread tin. Place in a large plastic bag and leave in a warm place for about an hour until doubled in size.

3 Preheat the oven to 200°C/fan oven 180°C/gas mark 6. Bake the loaf for 30–35 minutes until risen and golden. To check whether it is cooked, tip it out onto a wire cooling rack and knock the base with your knuckles. The loaf should sound hollow. Cool on the rack.

Home & Country
1957

Quick brown bread

12 oz. wholemeal flour, 2 level teaspoons salt, 4 oz. plain flour, ½ oz. yeast, ½ pint lukewarm water

Sift the flour and salt into a warm basin. Whisk the yeast with the liquid and add to the flour. Mix to a dough, turn onto a floured board and knead for ten minutes. Shape into two loaves or place in floured bread tins. Stand in a warm place until doubled in size. Bake in a hot oven 450 F for 10–15 minutes. Reduce heat to 400 F and continue baking in a moderate oven, approximately for 25 minutes.

Pork Pies

As the country began to recover from the years of deprivation and hardship, WI cooks began to rediscover the pleasures of traditional pastimes, recipes and cooking skills that had been in abeyance – a picnic in the British countryside was a perfect family day out in the late fifties. A raft of locally produced WI recipe books appeared with recipe ideas for all kinds of occasions and this recipe from East Kent for individual little pies would have been ideal for a family outing. The car would be packed with a rug, flask of tea, hard-boiled eggs and, of course, a good home-made cake as the family headed off to the great outdoors. Our updated recipe for Pork Pies has been adapted from The WI Book of Pastry.

Serves 8 · Preparation 30 minutes · Cook 30–40 minutes

Hot water crust pastry:
350g plain flour
1 tsp salt
150g lard
150ml milk and water, mixed

Filling:
350g lean pork
1 tbsp chopped fresh sage
3 tbsp stock or water
2 hard-boiled free-range eggs, shelled and sliced
salt and freshly ground black pepper
beaten egg, to glaze

1 Preheat the oven to 200°C/fan oven 180°C/gas mark 6. Sift the flour and salt together. Put the lard and liquid into a small pan and heat gently until the lard is melted, then bring to boil. Pour the mixture into the dry ingredients in one go and mix well to form a soft dough. Turn onto a floured work surface and knead lightly. Cover with a cloth to keep warm while preparing the filling.

2 Mince or chop the meat, season well and mix in the herbs and stock. Cut the pastry into eight portions. Reserve a quarter of each portion of pastry for a lid and with your hands mould the remainder by hand around the base of a tumbler to form a cup. The pastry should be about 1cm thick. Fill with the meat, adding a layer of sliced egg in the centre, and brush the edges with beaten egg. Roll out the reserved pastry as a lid and cover the pie. Repeat to make eight pies.

4 Brush each pie with a little egg and make a small steam hole. Place the pies on a baking sheet and bake for 30-40 minutes until golden and the meat is cooked. Cool and chill until ready to serve.

Personal Recipes, East Kent Federation 1957

Raised crust pastry (twelve ounces flour)

Filling: Threequarters pound lean pork, two/three hard boiled eggs, pepper and salt, a little stock or water, egg to glaze. Oven 380-400 F.
Chop the pork finely and add the seasoning. Cut eggs into slices. Make the pastry and cut into eight small portions. Mould each piece by hand or around the base of a tumbler. Fill and cover with a lid. Make a hole in each pie and then coat with a little egg. Bake for 30-40 minutes.
Each pie can be bound with a strip of greaseproof until nearly cooked in order to give support.

Cherry and Almond Cake

Farming concerns and rural issues have been at the heart of the campaigning arm of the WI since its inception. One very effective tool for publicising rural issues was broadcast five evenings a week from 1951. BBC Radio 4's The Archers, that 'everyday story of country folk', featured the WI from the start, with key characters such as the young Jill Archer attending meetings. BBC producers frequently contacted the NFWI for ideas and subject matter for storylines, and local recipes and cooking have always played an important role in The Archers, from competitive baking and preserving to Freda Fry's pies and puddings served at the Bull, and now a new generation of Ambridge women has started to attend WI meetings. Here's a cake from the Yorkshire WI recipe book Through Yorkshire's Kitchen Door, that Jill is sure to have rustled up in her Aga...

Makes 1 x 20cm cake · Preparation 15 minutes · Cook 1–1¼ hours

125g butter
125g caster sugar
2 large free-range eggs
pinch of salt
200g plain flour
1 tsp baking powder
50g ground almonds
50g glacé cherries, rinsed, dried
   and halved
2–3 tbsp milk, to mix

1 Preheat the oven to 180°C/fan oven 160°C/gas mark 4. Butter and base-line a deep 20cm round cake tin. Cream the butter and sugar together in a mixing bowl until pale and light. Beat the eggs with the salt and gradually add to the creamed mixture.

2 Sift together the flour and baking powder and fold it into the creamed mixture along with the ground almonds, in two batches. Then fold in the cherries (toss them in a little flour first, to stop them sinking to the bottom of the cake), adding milk as required to make a soft mixture.

3 Spoon into the prepared tin and level the surface. Bake for 1 hour until the cake is risen and golden and a skewer emerges from the centre of the cake clean and dry. Turn onto a wire rack to cool.

Through Yorkshire's Kitchen Door 1956

Cherry and almond cake

Ingredients: *4 oz butter, 4 oz sugar, 2 eggs, Salt, 7 oz flour, 1 tsp baking powder, 2 oz ground almonds, 2 oz glace cherries, little milk to mix*

Method: *Cream butter and sugar. Beat eggs with a pinch of salt and add gradually to the creamed mixture. Add flour, baking powder and ground almonds gradually, also cherries cut in half and lightly floured. Add milk as required to make a fairly moist mixture. Bake in a slow to moderate oven for one and a quarter hours to one and three quarter hours. Can be covered with white icing and decorated with cherries and almonds when cold.*
BRAMHOPE W Yorks

Pizza Margherita

Pizza has been with us for far longer than many modern readers might think. London has played host to a thriving Italian community since the 18th century, and restaurants such as Bertorelli's and Quaglino's became popular after the First World War. Perhaps surprisingly to modern readers, cooking pizza at home was also the norm, with recipes appearing in WI publications of the late 1950s, including The Berkshire Cookery Book. *It made a simple family supper well within the reach of the accomplished bakers of the WI.*

In her introduction to the book, Doris Cumming reports with no little horror that 'it may be thought that, in the future, pre-packed and prepared food will replace the individuality of home-cooking'. Although she is aware that these 'have a place in the running of a busy home', she asserts that 'by fostering good standards of home cooking... one has some means of comparison and discrimination'.

Makes 4 pizzas · Preparation 15 minutes, plus proving · Cook 12–15 minutes

500g Italian 00 flour or strong white bread flour
1½ tsp salt
2 tsp easy-blend yeast
2 tbsp olive oil
250g tomato passata
230g mozzarella
any extra toppings that you like, such as basil, anchovies, etc.

1 Sift the flour and salt into a mixing bowl and stir in the yeast. Whisk the oil with 300ml warm water and add to the flour. Mix to a soft dough and turn onto a lightly floured surface. Knead for 10 minutes until smooth and elastic. Place in a clean oiled bowl and cover with oiled cling film. Leave in a warm corner of the kitchen for 45 minutes or until doubled in size.

2 Preheat the oven to 220°C/fan oven 200°C/gas mark 7. Turn the dough out onto a floured surface and knead lightly to knock out any air. Divide into four and roll out to really thin circles about 2cm thick. Transfer to floured baking sheets.

3 Spread the passata over the dough leaving a narrow border, then scatter with the mozzarella. Cover with cling wrap and leave to prove for 15 minutes until puffy. Bake in batches in the oven – you may be able to fit in two at once. Each pizza takes about 12–15 minutes: the top should be golden and bubbling and the dough crisp.

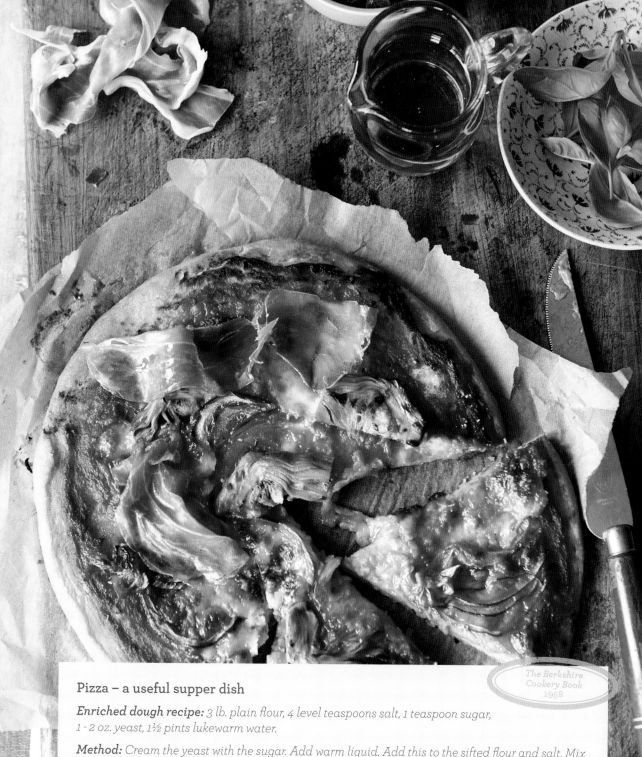

Pizza – a useful supper dish

Enriched dough recipe: *3 lb. plain flour, 4 level teaspoons salt, 1 teaspoon sugar, 1 - 2 oz. yeast, 1½ pints lukewarm water.*

Method: *Cream the yeast with the sugar. Add warm liquid. Add this to the sifted flour and salt. Mix all together Knead well. Set to rise.*
While dough is rising, lightly cook in a little fat, slices of tomato, onions and chopped herbs for three or four minutes. Cool and drain. Press dough into a large sandwich tin to about one inch in depth. Cover with the tomato mixture. Sprinkle with cheese or cover with very finely sliced cheese and sliced olives and place three or four anchovy fillets on the top. Prove for ten minutes. Glaze with a little melted butter. Bake for twenty to thirty minutes at 350 Fahr.

Beef Curry

WI members knew their curries. A way of life came to an end for many expatriates in 1947 with the Indian Independence Act, but they brought home their knowledge of cooking with spices and love for the dishes of the country they left behind. Curry recipes abound throughout WI publications, and an article from Home & Country *magazine August 1963 shows impressive understanding: 'Curry is, of course, not a specific dish but a whole class of cookery... recipes are innumerable, methods infinitely various'.*

The style of curry in the original recipe will be familiar to expats who remember the ubiquitous 'curry lunch', served in compounds and messes throughout the Middle and Far East.

Serves 4 · Preparation 15 minutes · Cook 1½ hours

2 tbsp vegetable oil
1 medium onion, finely chopped
1–2 cloves garlic, chopped
800g stewing beef, cut into cubes
2 tbsp curry powder
½ tsp salt
½ tsp freshly ground
    black pepper
1 tsp ground ginger
2 tbsp soy sauce, to taste
500ml beef stock or hot water
2 tbsp raisins
1 small eating apple, peeled,
    cored and diced

1   Heat the oil in a heavy-based pan. Add the onion and garlic and cook for 5 minutes until soft. Add the beef and brown on all sides. Stir in the curry powder and cook for a minute, then add salt, pepper and ginger. Mix well.

2   Add soy sauce and stock. Bring to the boil, cover and cook gently until tender (about 1½ hours). Add more water if it looks dry. Add raisins and apple. Serve with rice and chutney.

*Home & Country
1963*

Briefly, it can be described as food often combining sweet-and-sour and flavoured with a mixture of eastern spices (not necessarily fiery). Recipes are innumerable, methods infinitely various. Readers who want to learn more will find Mrs. Balbi Singh's Indian Cookery very helpful (Mills & Boon 21s.).

Curried beef
Ideally, curry powder should be made for each dish with fresh spices. But at least we can start with a tin we have not had for more than a fortnight.

Ingredients (for 6): *4 dessertspoonfuls curry powder, 1 clove garlic, 2–3 tablespoonfuls cooking oil, 1 teaspoonful salt, ½ teaspoonful ground black pepper, 2 lbs. beef cut into small cubes, 2 small onions, 3 tablespoonfuls soya sauce, 1 cup stock or hot water, 1 tablespoon cornflour, 4 tablespoonful stoned raisins and one apple (large)*

Heat oil in heavy pan. Stir in curry powder and when blended add crushed garlic, salt, pepper and ginger. Mix well. Add the meat, chopped onion and raisins. Stir and cook until the onion is soft. Add the soya sauce and water or stock. Bring to boiling point and cook gently until even and soft (about 5 minutes). Add the cubed apple. Mix the cornflour with a little water and stir into the meat mixture. Serve with rice and chutney.

Three Fruit Marmalade

WI members have always been enthusiastic and accomplished jam makers – the movement has been known by its 'jam and Jerusalem' image, despite working hard to dispel that rather one-dimensional view.

The booklet's original recipe makes marmalade with cooked fruit pulp. Nowadays we tend to prefer a clearer finish so this recipe is based on one in Best Kept Secrets of the WI: Jams, Pickles and Chutneys by Midge Thomas, where the fruit is squeezed first.

Makes about 2kg · Preparation 1 hour · Cook 2–2½ hours

750g citrus fruit – roughly
   1 grapefruit, 2 lemons and
   1 orange, scrubbed
1.5kg granulated sugar

1 Halve the fruit and squeeze out the juice. Remove the pips and membrane from the fruit halves and tie in a muslin bag. Cut the peel into even-sized thick or thin shreds, with a knife, or using a mincer or food processor.

2 Place the peel, muslin bag and squeezed juice in a preserving pan. Add 1.4 litres cold water and bring to the boil. Simmer gently, uncovered, for 1½–2 hours until the peel is tender and the contents of the pan reduced by half.

3 Remove the pan from heat, remove the bag and squeeze it hard between two plates to remove all the gooey liquid; this contains the pectin and is important for a good set.

4 Add the sugar and stir until completely dissolved. Quickly bring to the boil, and test for setting point after 10 minutes (see page 86). Remove scum with a spoon and cool the marmalade for 5–10 minutes, until a skin forms.

5 Stir the marmalade gently and pour it into warmed sterilised jars. Seal, label and store in a cool, dark place.

Guide to Preservation 1964

Three Fruit Marmalade

2 grapefruit, 4 lemons, 2 oranges = 3 lbs. fruit, 6 lbs. sugar, 6 pints water

Method: *Scrub fruit, boil for 3 minutes. Peel and remove pith. Cut peel into shreds. Remove pips and tie with pith in muslin bag. Chop pulp. Simmer peel, pulp, and acid with muslin bag in the water for 1½–2 hours until shreds are tender and contents reduced by a third. Take off heat, squeeze and remove bag, add warmed sugar, stir until dissolved. Boil. Test for setting point after 10 minutes. Remove scum. Leave for 5–10 minutes. Stir gently and pour into warmed jars, fill to the brim. Cover, label and store in a dark ventilated place.*

Refrigerator Cookies

Despite the arrival of fridges on the wider domestic market by the 1950s, they were still rare enough for a new acquisition to be cause for celebration – by 1962 still only a third of British households owned one. Writing for Home & Country *in June 1965, Margaret Ryan opened her feature on 'You and Your Refrigerator' with a revealing paragraph: 'On that exciting and delightful day when we first see our very own refrigerator in our very own kitchen, our minds almost certainly turn first to the ice cubes... and to the joy of keeping milk, meat, stock and so on without the dread that the cautious sniff will meet the unmistakable smell of "going off"!'*

She goes on to add advice on other uses that might not immediately come to mind, including this smart idea – chilled cookie dough that can be kept in the fridge and sliced and baked on demand (adapted from the recipe in The WI Book of Biscuits*).*

Home & Country
1965

Makes 8–10 · Preparation 15 minutes · Cook 15–20 minutes

200g plain flour
1 tsp baking powder
pinch of salt
200g caster sugar
100g butter, melted
1 medium free-range egg,
   beaten
flavouring – see variations
   below

1 Sift the flour into a bowl with the baking powder and the salt. Stir in the sugar and any flavouring then add the cooled melted butter and the egg. Mix to a soft dough. Turn onto a lightly floured surface and knead lightly into a sausage shape 5cm in diameter. Wrap in baking parchment and then foil and store in the fridge or freezer until needed.

2 Preheat the oven to 180°C/fan oven 160°C/gas mark 4. If your cookie mix is in the freezer, bring to room temperature to allow it to soften. Cut off slices 0.5cm thick and place on greased baking sheets with room to spread. Bake for 15–20 minutes until golden. Cool on the tray for 5 minutes then transfer to wire cooling racks until cold.

Variations:
· 1 tsp vanilla essence and 150g chopped dark chocolate
· 1 tsp ground ginger and 50g chopped stem ginger
· 1 tbsp instant coffee powder and 50g chopped walnuts
· grated rind of 1 lemon and 50g currants or dried cranberries
· replace caster sugar with soft brown sugar and add 1 tsp vanilla and 50g raisins

Herrings in Oatmeal

A colourful illustrated WI booklet called The Balancing Act – Food for Health and Happiness *appeared in 1962. Chapters covered topics such as 'The Foods we need and how they work'. This was the WI in full education mode. The first sentence on the opening page reads 'If food isn't fun, there's something wrong!' The housewife is encouraged to add variety, to bring food 'alive'. 'You may say "Easier said than done" but with the shops fuller than ever before of... all the world produces, it can be a fascinating game.'*

Fish is one of the 'outstanding foods' our challenged mum should include in her family's diet. 'Fish of every kind, fresh, smoked, tinned and dried is an invaluable source of protein... calcium and Vitamin B'.

This classically simple dish is one of the best ways to serve herrings. Get the fishmonger to bone out the fish for you. Serve for breakfast with grilled bacon or as a main meal with new potatoes and kale or broccoli.

Serves 4 · Preparation 15 minutes · Cook 20 minutes

4 herrings, filleted
milk
100g medium oatmeal
1 tbsp sunflower or rapeseed oil, for frying
salt and freshly ground black pepper

1 Dip the herrings in milk on a dinner plate and season well. Put the oatmeal on a large plate and dip the herrings into it to coat on both sides, pressing the oatmeal on with your hands.

2 Heat the oil in a heavy-based frying pan over a medium heat and cook the fish first on one side then the other (3–5 minutes in total) until the oatmeal is golden and the fish just cooked. Serve on warm plates with lemon wedges.

WI Recipe Book 1965

Nutty Herrings

Ingredients: (for 4) 4 herrings, coarse oatmeal, salt, little fat for frying

Method: Bone herrings. Rub in a little salt. Coat with oatmeal and press well on with knife. Melt very little fat in pan. Cook first on one side then the other (about 15 minutes all told). To serve, Mustard Sauce is a good addition. If liked herrings can be baked on a greased dish in a hot oven, instead of frying.

Baked Eggs with Spinach

Surrey Federation Chairman Joan Lash was obviously a forward thinker. In her introduction to The Surrey Chicken, *published in 1965, she looked ahead to the new millennium. 'The year 2000 is rushing towards us' she wrote, 'we hear of automation for this and that, but surely as long as women are women, there is one aspect... in which they will always want to have a hand... the preparation of food'. The encompassing nature of that role is summed up in the topics covered – luxury dishes for the single-handed hostess, cooking for the invalid tray, supper dishes and so on.*

We've chosen to update this supper dish by baking the eggs rather than hard-boiling them first – making them lighter to eat. You could top the dish with a ready-made cheese sauce as in the original recipe but cream and grated Parmesan are simpler.

Serves 2 or 4 as a starter · Preparation 15 minutes · Cook 10–12 minutes

450g fresh spinach, washed
25g butter
freshly grated nutmeg
4 large free-range eggs
4 tbsp double cream
4 tbsp freshly grated Parmesan
salt and freshly ground black
   pepper

1 Preheat the oven to 190°C/fan oven 170°C/gas mark 5. Tear the spinach leaves from their stalks and place in a large pan with any water from washing. Cook, covered for a couple of minutes until the spinach is wilted. Drain thoroughly, pressing out any excess liquid and then return to the pan with half the butter, nutmeg and seasoning. Mix well.

2 Divide the spinach between two buttered shallow gratin dishes (or four large ramekins). Make a well in the spinach, break in the eggs and season. Spoon over the cream. Sprinkle with Parmesan and dot with the remaining butter. Bake for 10–12 minutes until the eggs are just set. Serve with crispy bread to mop up any juices.

The Surrey Chicken 1965

Eggs with spinach
Chop cooked spinach and put in an oven dish. Make wells in the spinach in which to place whole or halved hard boiled eggs. Cover with a cheese sauce. Heat under grill as required.   Burstow W.I.

WI members enjoying lunch on the steps of the Albert Memorial
opposite the Royal Albert Hall during the NFWI AGM,
1971

1966–1975

The swinging decade

With London 'swinging', and the country seemingly obsessed with mini skirts, the Beatles and all things psychedelic, it might be thought by modern readers that the WI in the late 1960s was in danger of turning into an organisation for out-of-touch country dwellers.

Minutes from AGMs of the period reveal something rather different. A resolution was passed at the 1971 AGM changing the interpretation of the WI's non-party political and non-sectarian rules, so that women could take a stance on politically significant issues. In 1974 nearly half a million members in a record-breaking 9,309 WIs expressed their concerns about the availability of habit-forming drugs to young people, campaigned for free family planning with the arrival of the Pill, and pleaded for a national policy for reclamation, reuse and recycling of waste. In 1975 equality 'of opportunity and legal status' for women was high on the agenda. But the business of daily life and its challenges continued in the background and, as ever, *Home & Country* magazine reflected both aspects. The contents page from January 1970 tells the story in a nutshell. Articles on 'Drug Business', sex education in primary schools, the value of hedgerow trees, and 'Denman comes of age' appear alongside exploding bed-warmers, indoor gardens, 'dark thoughts' on motoring, and that old chestnut – the need for weight-watching 'after the feasting'. In the sixties and seventies package holidays revolutionised travel, and French food was all the rage. Food writer Elizabeth David, according to her biographer Artemis Cooper, 'transformed the eating habits of middle-class England'. She had spent the war years living abroad and, on returning to the UK, was horrified at the bad food and dreary lives of post-war Britain. Her iconic cookery books and

newspaper columns were published in the early fifties, but only now was her influence to filter through into all walks of life. She inspired a revolution against the supposed bland food and meagre rations of the previous decades, ironically at the same time as the WI's ongoing efforts to safeguard regional recipes. (But Elizabeth herself recognised the importance of the WI's work in her later book *English Bread and Yeast Cookery*, published in 1977.)

During this decade a new collectible part-work magazine, *The Cordon Bleu Cookery Course*, ran for more than 72 weeks 'bringing the continental touch to our English cooking'. New kitchen equipment such as electric mixers (the iconic A701 Kenwood Chef had arrived in 1960) and food mills promised short cuts for the cook, but WI members were still warned (in the pages of *H&C*) that they should 'Use them to help you, not to replace you'.

Left image
HM Queen Elizabeth the Queen Mother at the WI stand at the Royal Show

Right image
WI members visiting young patients in hospital, 1969

Crêpes Suzette

The wonders of eggs were celebrated by the members of Hertfordshire WI in a little booklet of recipes, Get Cracking, *in 1967. As Helen MacInnes, chairman of the federation at the time, wrote in her introduction, an egg 'can be eaten, drunk, used as a hair lotion, a face pack, or Granny's embrocation; it is a symbol of Spring and of Easter, and still poses the eternal problem of Which Came First'. Recipes ranged from a basic omelette to Oeufs Farcies aux Crevettes and this Sixties classic, Crêpes Suzette.*

Many readers may recall the drama of sitting in a restaurant dining room in the late Sixties or early Seventies, as the formally attired maître d'hotel wheeled a trolley with a gas ring to the table and enacted the ritual of preparing and flambéing this classic dessert. The sense of theatre was enjoyed by all, the worry of whether an inexperienced practitioner might singe his fringe, or the caramel sauce would burn was part of the fun.

Serves 4 (makes about 8 crêpes) · Preparation 20 minutes · Cook 15 minutes

For the pancake batter:
125g plain flour
pinch of salt
25g caster sugar
2 medium free-range eggs
300ml semi-skimmed milk
butter, for frying

For the sauce:
50g unsalted butter
50g caster sugar
1 tbsp each grated orange and
   lemon rind
juice of 1 orange
2 tbsp orange liqueur such as
   Cointreau or Grand Marnier
3 tbsp brandy or rum

1   Follow the original recipe method to make the crêpes. They can be made in advance and reheated!

*Get Cracking
1967*

For the crêpes:
2 eggs
4 oz. plain flour, sifted
1 dstspn. caster sugar
½ pint milk
pinch of salt
butter or oil for cooking

For the sauce:
3 oz. unsalted butter
1 tbspn. grated lemon rind
1 tbspn. grated orange rind
juice of 1 orange
3 oz. caster sugar
2 tbspn. Cointreau
3 tbspn. rum or brandy

Place the flour, sugar and salt in a basin. Make a well in the centre and add the eggs and a little milk. Stir, drawing in the flour from the sides, beat until smooth. Add the rest of the milk gradually, beating well. Transfer the batter to a jug. Melt a little butter in a frying pan, pour in just enough batter to coat the pan. When the underside is brown, turn it over and cook on the other side. Turn out onto a warm plate and keep hot. Repeat with the remaining batter. To make the sauce, melt the butter in an omelette pan, add the sugar, lemon and orange rind, orange juice and Cointreau and bring to the boil. Put 3 crêpes into the pan, basting frequently. When hot, fork into quarters, and repeat with the remaining crêpes. Warm the brandy or rum, pour over the hot crêpes in the pan and set alight. Serve immediately with the remaining sauce.

Chocolate Mousse

March 1967 and Margaret Ryan was 'Cooking with Chocolate' in the pages of Home & Country.
*She advises that although a 'universal favourite, the handling of chocolate is tricky'. But she suggests
this is all down to 'mistakes in temperature and mixing'. Her advice on avoiding these problems reveals
her skill of food writing at its best – practical but evocative with a clear personal voice. She writes:
'Chocolate contains cocoa butter which responds sharply to too high a temperature... it must be melted
over indirect heat – that is, in a basin over hot water. Be sure that the upper part does not touch the
water. Steam should be prevented from entering the chocolate.' Most sensibly, she goes on: 'You should
be able to hold the basin in your hand, but it should feel hot. Before use it should be cooled to blood heat
– that is a temperature that is neither hot or cold to an experimental finger.'*

These days we prefer a mousse without added sugar so the recipe has been adapted accordingly.

Serves 4–6 · Preparation 15 minutes, plus 6–12 hours chilling

225g dark chocolate, broken
   into pieces
1 tbsp rum (optional)
4 large free-range eggs,
   separated

1 Place the chocolate in a basin with 4 tbsp cold water
and set over a pan of hot water. Do not let the water boil.
It's better just to leave the chocolate for longer to melt
slowly. Or heat it in the microwave on a medium setting
in 30 second blasts, stirring between each. Remember
that microwaved food continues to cook, so remove it
when the chocolate is half melted and leave to stand, then
stir till smooth. Stir in the rum (if using).

2 Let the chocolate cool to blood heat (see original),
then beat in the egg yolks one at a time. Whisk the whites
until stiff but not dry and stir a quarter quickly into the
chocolate to loosen the mixture. Add the chocolate to the
remaining whites and fold together quickly and lightly.
Spoon into individual glasses or ramekins and chill for at
least 6 hours or overnight.

Chocolate Mousse

*Home & Country
1967*

*(enough for 4 to 6) 4 oz. plain chocolate; 4 oz. castor sugar; 4 eggs
Dissolve the chocolate over hot water and add the sugar. Stir until uniform. Separate
the yolks from the whites of the eggs and add the yolks beaten until pale and foamy, a
tablespoonful at a time. (Make sure the chocolate is no more than blood heat.) Whip
the whites with a pinch of cream of tartar until they are standing stiffly in peaks which
you cannot shake down. (The cream of tartar helps to stabilize the foam.) Fold them
very, very lightly into the chocolate mixture. Pour into a soufflé dish and let it stand for
at least 12 hours before serving.*

Duck à l'Orange

In his television series, Heston's Feasts, the eponymous chef acknowledged Duck à l'Orange as a Sixties classic. So the WI were right on track when this recipe found its way into The WI Book of Party Recipes *(1969). Though some of the more bizarre party dishes deserve to be left in the 'swinging' decade, this recipe is well worth serving today.*

Serves 3–4 · Preparation 15 minutes · Cook 1–1½ hours

1 duck, about 1.5–1.7kg, rinsed and patted dry with kitchen paper
25g butter
2 large oranges
25g granulated sugar
1 tbsp red wine vinegar
300ml chicken stock, ideally fresh but a cube will do
50ml port
salt, celery salt and freshly ground black pepper

1   Preheat the oven to 200°C/fan oven 180°C/gas mark 6. Prick the duck skin all over with a fork. Loosen skin around the neck and push butter up inside. Season and place in a roasting tin. Roast for 1–1½ hours, basting during cooking.

2   While the duck is cooking, make the sauce. Prepare the oranges as in the original recipe. A swivel-bladed peeler is the best tool for removing the skin. For the caramel, dissolve the sugar in 2–3 tbsp cold water in a small pan over a very low heat, then boil and cook until golden brown. Add vinegar, stock and port and simmer for 15 minutes. Set aside.

3   Remove duck from the oven and leave to rest on a warm plate. Drain fat from the tin and add a little sauce, scraping up any juices. Return this to the sauce with the orange strips and juice. Warm orange segments in the oven. Carve the duck and arrange on warm plates. Spoon over segments then spoon over sauce with orange peel. Serve with peas.

The WI Book of Party Recipes 1969

Duck à l'orange

1 duck, about 3–4 lb, 1 onion, 1 carrot, 2 oranges, 4 oz. butter, 1 oz. flour, 5–6 lumps sugar, 1 tbspn vinegar, ½ glass port, seasoning, celery salt

Method: *Draw and truss the duck. Remove wishbone. Cover with butter, season and place in a roasting pan. Prepare sauce. Melt 2 oz. butter and brown the giblets, add sliced carrot and onion and brown. Stir in flour, brown, add 1 pint water and bring to the boil. Season, add celery salt and simmer for 1–2 hours. Strain into a pan. Peel skin off oranges thinly, without pith. Cut into thin julienne and blanch in boiling water for 2–3 minutes. Drain, refresh and set aside. Cut remaining pith off oranges, cut out segments. Squeeze pith to extract juice, and set juice and segments aside. Place sugar in pan with 2–3 tbspns water and boil to caramel, add vinegar. Add this to sauce gradually, tasting well. Add port and cook for 10–15 minutes. Skim. Roast duck in a hot oven (Reg. 6 or 400F) for approx 1 hour, basting well. Remove and keep warm. Drain fat from pan and add some sauce to deglaze. Return all to saucepan, add strips of peel and juice from oranges. Warm segments in oven. Arrange carved duck on warm dish. Place segments around, pour sauce and peel over. Do not add julienne to sauce more than ½–1 hour before serving or sauce will become bitter.*

Risotto Milanese

'Cooking Questions?' made a regular appearance as a column in Home & Country *throughout the decade. The answering recipe to the query below, from a reader, is charmingly and evocatively written and, even for more savvy cooks today, gives a detailed and user-friendly guide to making this classic risotto. Elizabeth David's* Italian Food *had first appeared back in 1955 and was now widely available in paperback but this lyrical recipe shows that H&C writers were well up to speed on their own. This version really stands as it is and barely needs adjusting.*

Serves 4 · Preparation 10 minutes · Cook 20 minutes

1.5 litres chicken or beef stock
50g butter
2 tbsp olive oil
1 medium onion, finely chopped
½ tsp saffron strands
350g arborio rice
100ml dry white wine
50g Parmesan, freshly grated
salt and freshly ground black
   pepper

1 Follow the method in the original recipe, but use 25g butter with the olive oil to cook the onion. Add the saffron strands when the onion is soft and before adding the rice. Continue as the original. You could serve the risotto with an Italian sausage such as luganega, or the classic Milanese way with bone marrow, which these days is even available at some supermarkets.

Home & Country
1970

A query from a reader writing from Italy:
When I make risotto at home it is quite dry – the rice grains separate and almost fluffy, and although it tastes good it does not compare with the risotto served in restaurants here, where the rice is softer and the consistency of the dish is creamy. My recipe seems the same and I use Patna-type rice. What makes the difference?
Answer: You are using the wrong rice. For an Italian risotto you need Italian rice, which can be bought in this country. It is pale yellow in colour and it is more expensive than other types of rice.

Risotto alla Milanese

Ingredients (to serve 4–6):

3 pints chicken stock (made from bouillon cubes if necessary), 1 medium onion, finely chopped, 4 oz. butter, 1 lb. Italian rice, 1 wineglassfull white wine, 2 oz. grated Parmesan cheese, salt.

You must give risotto all your attention for the half-hour or so it takes to cook. You must have a really large pan to cook it in – one holding 3 quarts is not too big. (A frequent cause of failure in cooking rice is that it cannot move freely.) You must also have a second pan for the stock and sufficient space on the top of your cooker to keep two pans simultaneously on the heat. Have a pint measure at hand.

Bring the chicken stock to the boil. Keep it gently simmering over a low heat all the time you are cooking. In the big pan dissolve 2 oz. butter and in it gently cook the onion until it is soft. Add the rice all at once and turn it about with a long handled spoon until it is glistening with butter. Pour in the wine and let it bubble rapidly until it has almost disappeared. Ladle in a pint of simmering stock onto the rice and let it simmer, stirring from time to time, until the liquid is all absorbed. Add a second pint of stock and again cook gently until it is all absorbed. Now proceed cautiously, adding the simmering stock a few tablespoonfuls at a time until the rice is quite tender and the liquid nearly but not quite absorbed. Do not let the rice become mushy. Test by tasting. The moment you are satisfied the rice is cooked stop adding liquid. Now season carefully with salt and pepper, tasting critically. Take the remaining butter which should be soft and stir it into the rice with a fork. Finally fork in the grated cheese. Serve very hot on very hot plates.

'People are so friendly; I've expanded my horizons and met new people of all ages.'
Seven Hills WI member

Gingered Forehock of Bacon

In the 1930s Danish imports had accounted for over 60 per cent of the bacon eaten in the UK. Even in 1970, despite campaigns promoting our own pigs, British bacon was hard to come by. Margaret Ryan made a plea for local butchers to stock British bacon in a feature for Home & Country. *But, sadly, 'I try mostly in vain', she says. The WI has always campaigned on behalf of British farmers, and continues to do so, to raise awareness of issues such as how pigs are farmed outside the UK, and to highlight our own high standards of welfare.*

Serves 6 · Preparation 20 minutes, plus soaking overnight · Cook 1¾ hours

1.75kg English smoked bacon joint
2 sprigs fresh rosemary
300ml ginger ale
100g demerara sugar
1 tsp English mustard powder
2 pieces stem ginger, finely chopped

1 Place the joint in a large container and cover with cold water. Leave to soak for six hours or overnight. The next day remove it from the water and place in a pan, as in the original recipe, with the ginger ale and rosemary.

2 Preheat the oven to 200°C/fan oven 180°C/gas mark 6. Follow the original recipe and remove the skin and cover the fat with the ginger and mustard paste. Roast the joint for 15 minutes until the coating is golden. Leave it to rest for at least 15 minutes before carving.

Home & Country
1970

Gingered Forehock of Bacon

To serve 6: *4 lb. piece of smoked forehock; 1 tablespoonful dried rosemary, or 1 good sprig fresh rosemary; 1 small bottle ginger ale; 4 oz. demerara sugar; 1 level teaspoonful dry mustard; 2 teaspoonfuls chopped stem ginger.*

Soak the forehock for six hours or overnight. Put it in a large pan and pour the ginger ale over it. If it does not cover the joint, make up the level with water. Add the rosemary. Bring slowly to the boil and simmer gently for 1½ hours. Drain the joint, keeping back a small cupful of the liquid. When the joint is cool enough to handle, strip off the skin, being careful not to tear it. With a sharp knife lightly score the fat in a diamond pattern. Mix the dry mustard, sugar and ginger into a thick paste with a little of the liquid you kept from the pan. Spread the paste over the fat, pressing it in with the back of a spoon. Put it in a hot oven – 450F, mark 7 – for 15 minutes.

Orchard Chutney

In September 1970 Rosemary Wadey was introduced as the new cookery writer for Home & Country, *a position she would hold into the new century. With a background as a cook-manageress and time spent at the Good Housekeeping Institute, Rosemary began her WI career with a feature on using home-grown vegetables and fruit in chutneys and pickles. This is one of her first recipes.*

Makes 1.3kg · Preparation 30 minutes · Cook 3 hours

1kg plums, washed, halved
    and stoned
1kg red tomatoes, sliced
1 litre malt vinegar
2 cloves garlic, peeled
500g onions, peeled and
    quartered
1.2kg cooking apples, peeled,
    cored and roughly chopped
125g sultanas
125g currants
500g demerara sugar
1 tsp salt
2 tbsp pickling spices, tied
    in muslin

1   Place the plums, tomatoes and vinegar together in a large heavy-based pan or preserving pan and simmer gently for about 1 hour until soft.

2   Place the garlic, onions, apples, sultanas and currants in a processor and pulse until chopped. Add to the plum mixture with the sugar, salt and spices. Heat gently to dissolve the sugar then simmer over a low heat, stirring occasionally, until tender and thick enough to leave a trail when you run a wooden spoon through the centre of the pan. This will take about 2 hours.

3   Pot the chutney in warm sterile jars filled to the brim. Cover with vinegar resistant tops. Leave to cool, then label and store in a cool, dark place. Chutney matures in flavour and should ideally be left for at least 6 months before eating.

*Home & Country
1970*

Orchard Chutney

2 lb. plums, 2 lb. red tomatoes, peeled and sliced, 1½ pints malt vinegar, ½ oz. unpeeled garlic, 1 lb. onions, peeled, 2½ lb. cooking apples, peeled and cored, 4 oz. sultanas, 4 oz. currants, 1 lb. demerara sugar, 2 oz. salt, 1 ½ tablespoonfuls pickling spices, tied in muslin

Wash the plums; cut in half and remove the stones if they are the freestone variety, if not leave whole. Place plums, tomatoes and vinegar in a large pan and simmer gently till soft. Remove plum stones if not already done. Mince the peeled garlic, onions, apples and dried fruit and add to the plum mixture with the sugar, salt and pickling spices. Bring to the boil and simmer gently, uncovered, until tender and well reduced. This takes about 2 hours. Remove spice bag. Pot and cover.

Seafood Provençale

Although this decade witnessed the explosion of cheap package holidays to Europe, families still continued to holiday at home, and caravanning was very popular. The spiral bound WI Indoor/Outdoor Cookbook was a dual-purpose publication. Open it on one side and it is aimed at those who enjoy cooking outdoors – 'afloat, caravanning and camping' recipes. Turn it over and you're holding another book altogether, covering budget meals, quick dishes and living alone. We've chosen Scampi Provençale from the quick dishes. You can buy good-quality seafood mixes, plus excellent fresh fish stock, which make it even easier to prepare.

Serves 2 · Preparation 5 minutes · Cook 10 minutes

1 tbsp olive oil
15g butter
1 medium onion, chopped
1 clove garlic, crushed
2 fresh bay leaves
¼ tsp saffron strands
225g can chopped Italian
   tomatoes
50ml dry white wine
   (or fish stock)
300g uncooked mixed seafood,
   fresh or frozen
salt and freshly ground black
   pepper

1 Heat the oil and butter in a medium pan and cook the onion for 5 minutes until softened. Add the garlic, bay leaves and saffron and cook for a minute. Stir in the chopped tomatoes and wine.

2 Bring to the boil and simmer gently for 5 minutes. Then add the seafood, bring to the boil and simmer gently for a couple of minutes until cooked through. Check seasoning and discard the bay leaves. Serve in warm dishes with steamed rice.

The WI Indoor/
Outdoor Cookbook
1972

Scampi Provençale

Menu
Avocado Pear Vinaigrette
Scampi Provencale
Dessert Apple

4 oz packet frozen scampi, thawed, 4 oz rice, 1½ oz butter, 1 small chopped onion, 2 tablespoons chopped green pepper, Garlic, 1 small can tomatoes (drained), 1/8 pint (4 tablespoons) dry white wine or cider

Put rice to cook in salted water. Using a thick based pan melt the butter and gently fry the onion, garlic and pepper for about 5 minutes. Add the chopped tomatoes and wine or cider. Add the scampi and cook for a further 5 minutes. Drain the rice when soft and mix with the scampi and serve while very hot.

Lemon Cheesecake

In 1974 the Derbyshire Federation of WIs produced a 96-page recipe book, 'in response to many requests from Home and Abroad... with families in mind, catering for all occasions... compiled to meet the challenge of a changing pattern of life'. The contents page vividly reflects family life in the Seventies, and chapters such as Meals for One or Two, Picnic and Caravan, 6 o'Clock Special, Watching the Budget and Sky's the Limit, offer us a compelling glimpse back in time.

Cheesecake was a seventies favourite, usually made with cream cheese and set with gelatine on a crushed biscuit base. To bring the recipe up-to-date we simply replaced the evaporated milk with whipped cream.

Serves 6 · Preparation 20 minutes, plus chilling

100g digestive biscuits
50g butter, melted
grated rind and juice of
    2 unwaxed lemons
2 sheets gelatine or 15g
    powdered gelatine
50g caster sugar
250g soft cheese
150ml whipping cream, lightly
    whipped
grated dark chocolate (and
    fresh raspberries if desired),
    to decorate

1 Crush the biscuits in a strong plastic bag using a rolling pin. Add them to the melted butter and press into the base of a 20cm loose-bottomed flan tin. Chill while you prepare the filling.

2 Make the lemon juice up to 150ml with warm water and pour over the sheets of gelatine in a shallow dish. Leave to soak for 5 minutes then heat gently in the microwave or sit the dish in a pan of simmering water to dissolve. Stir in the lemon rind and caster sugar.

3 Beat the cheese until soft then fold in the lemon mixture and the lightly whipped cream. Pour over the biscuit base and level the surface. Chill until set. To serve, remove the cheesecake from the flan tin and set on a serving plate. Arrange raspberries on the top (if using) and scatter with grated dark chocolate.

*Derbyshire WI
Recipe Book
1974*

Cheesecake

Ingredients: Biscuit base, 4oz digestive biscuits, (crushed), 2oz butter
Method: 1. Melt the butter in a pan over a low heat, add the crushed biscuits.
2. Mix well and press into an eight inch flan ring on serving dish and put in a cool place to set.
Filling: 8oz soft curd cheese, 2oz caster sugar, small tin evaporated milk (chilled), 2 lemons, ½ pack gelatine
Method: 1. Dissolve the gelatine in juice of two lemons made up to ¼ pint with warm water, add finely grated rind of lemons and caster sugar.
2. Whisk evaporated milk.
3. Blend lemon mixture with cheese and fold in evaporated milk.
4. Pour quickly into prepared flan case and smooth the surface with a hot knife. Chill.
5. Before serving remove flan ring and decorate with grated chocolate or as desired.

Devil's Food Cake

Another recipe from the Derbyshire WI Recipe Book of 1974 (see page 134), this cake appeared in the '6 o'Clock Special' chapter. Dark, moist, chocolate Devil's Food Cake originated in the US at the beginning of the 20th century, as a counterpoint to pale white Angel Cake, made from egg whites. Its presence in the Derbyshire book reflects the prevailing fascination with American youth culture, when popular TV programmes such as Happy Days, and films like Jaws and Grease, made us long for all things American.

This cake is sometimes known as Red Velvet Cake, the colour coming from the use of bicarbonate of soda and water, which brings out reddish tinges in cocoa. We now tend to add food colouring to accentuate the redness.

Makes one 20cm sandwich cake · Preparation 30 minutes · Cook 35 minutes

50g cocoa
225ml water
175g plain flour
¼ tsp baking powder
1 tsp bicarbonate of soda
100g butter or margarine
300g caster sugar
2 large free-range eggs, beaten

For the topping and filling:
100g soft butter or margarine
75g granulated sugar
4 tbsp milk
1 tbsp instant coffee mixed with
   1 tbsp boiling water
225g icing sugar
40g cocoa powder

1   Follow the method in the original recipe, using two 20cm sandwich cake tins and bake at 180°C/fan oven 160°C/gas mark 4. Cool and fill as instructed.

Derbyshire WI
Recipe Book
1974

Ingredients:
6oz plain flour
¼ teaspoon baking powder
1 flat teaspoon bicarbonate of soda
2oz cocoa
7 ½ fl oz water
4oz margarine
10oz caster sugar
2 eggs

Topping:
4oz soft margarine
3oz granulated sugar
4 tablespoons milk
1 tablespoon coffee essence
8oz icing sugar
3 level dessertspoons cocoa

Method: 1 Blend the cocoa and water.
2 Cream the fat and sugar. Add the beaten egg gradually.
3 Sift the flour, soda and baking powder. Fold alternately into the creamed mixture with the blended cocoa and water.
4 Divide between two lined and greased eight inch sandwich tins.
5 Bake at 350F, Regulo 4 for approximately 30–35 minutes.

Topping: 1 Melt the margarine in a pan. Stir in the sugar, making sure it doesn't burn. Add the milk and essence.
2 Bring to the boil, stirring continuously. Cool.
3 Add to the sifted icing sugar and cocoa. Beat well.
4 Cool until of a coating consistency or spreading consistency, as required, for filling and topping respectively.

Bara Brith

The first WI set up in Britain in 1915 was in the Welsh village, Llanfairpwll. Versions of Bara Brith make a regular appearance in earlier WI publications, reflecting Wales' strong presence within the WI – so much so, that for a period, Home & Country *magazine contained pages entirely in Welsh. As we are unlikely to want to make four loaves at a time, the updated recipe is scaled down.*

Makes 2 x 500g loaves · Preparation 30 minutes, plus rising · Cook 1–1½ hours

2 tsp dried yeast plus 1 tsp sugar

300ml warm milk

650g strong white bread flour, plus extra for dusting

1 tsp salt

1 tsp mixed spice

150g lard or butter, or a mixture of both

150g dark brown muscovado sugar

250g raisins

250g sultanas

150g currants

50g mixed peel

1 large free-range egg

1 Whisk the yeast and sugar into 75ml of the warm milk. Leave to stand in a warm place for 15 minutes until frothy.

2 Sieve the flour into a large bowl with the salt and spice. Rub in the fat until the mixture looks like breadcrumbs. Stir in the sugar and fruit. Whisk the egg with the remaining milk and add to the yeast mixture. Make a well in the centre, add the yeast liquid and mix to a soft dough.

3 Turn out onto a lightly floured surface and knead for 8–10 minutes until smooth. Return the dough to a lightly oiled clean bowl, cover with cling film and leave in a warm place to rise for 1½ hours or until twice its original size.

4 Preheat the oven to 180°C/fan oven 160°C/gas mark 4. Knead the dough lightly on a floured surface. Divide into two and shape into two fat sausages. Press into greased 500g loaf tins. Cover with oiled cling film and prove in a warm place for about 20 minutes. Bake for 1–1½ hours until risen and golden brown and the base sounds hollow when tapped.

WI Diamond Jubilee Cookbook 1975

Bara brith *Traditional Welsh recipe (makes four loaves)*

1½ oz yeast or ½ oz dried yeast (15 g) plus 1 teaspoon sugar, 1 pint warm milk (500 ml), 3 lb flour (1.3 kg), 12 oz lard or butter or mixed fat (300 g), 12 oz brown sugar (300 g), 2 level teaspoons salt (10 ml), 1 lb stoned raisins (400g), 2 lb mixed dried fruit (800 g), 4 oz peel (100 g), ½ teaspoon mixed spice (5 ml), 2-3 eggs

Put the yeast or dried yeast and sugar into ¼ pint (150 ml) of the warm milk. Sieve the flour into a warm basin. Rub in the fat. Add all dry ingredients. Make a well in the centre, add eggs and remaining warm milk to yeast liquid and use to mix to a soft dough. Knead. Cover and leave in a warm place to rise for 1½ hours or until twice its original size. Knead lightly on a floured board. Divide into four and put into greased tins (1 lb or ½ kg). Put to prove in a warm place for about 20 minutes. Bake at 350F (180C) Gas 4 for 1½-2 hours. When cold, slice as for bread and butter, thinly and butter well.

Campaigning WI members outside the NFWI AGM
at the Royal Albert Hall,
1983

1976–1985
Finding a balance

'About as effective as the Women's Institute.' So said the editor in her Comment column that opened the New Year issue of *Home & Country* in 1976. She viewed the statement as a 'taunt' that had been heard many times 'in our sixty years of existence'. She goes on to write, 'we do not enter lightly into controversy, and we do not hit the headlines every day', which sounds rather diffident for a spokeswoman for the largest women's voluntary organisation in the country. What was going on that this great British institution was starting to sound so apologetic?

The WI was struggling to find a balance between its achievements as a highly successful campaigning women's organisation and the widely held view of it as a cosy middle-class enclave. The 'jam and Jerusalem' image was – and still is, in many ways – a double-edged sword, representing both a celebration of the strengths of the WI, and a blinkered view that obscures its many triumphs as a social and practical network for women. (The book of that title was published in 1977.) In an era that would encompass the election of our first female prime minister, the miners' strike, the setting up of the Greenham Common peace camp in 1981 and the Falklands War, whatever the views of the public at large, the WI was certainly not merely the domain of the homely farmer's wife – if that had ever been the case.

As ever, the NFWI was doing what it had always done – quietly getting on with it. WIs worried about issues that are startlingly familiar to us today, revealing that, as ever, the movement was well ahead of its time. Alternative energy sources,

Keep fit demonstration as part of an healthy eating campaign outside the Royal Albert Hall during the NFWI AGM, 1984

more rented accommodation for homeless people, protecting children from the availability of pornographic and violent literature, single sex wards in hospitals, the provision of hospice care and the spread of Aids – all were among resolutions put forward to AGMs of the period.

And still life went on. Dinner parties, skateboards, supermarkets versus the village shop, Concorde's first commercial flight in 1976, a young Delia Smith on TV, chocolate profiteroles, Angel Delight and Smash – all were embraced by WI members with their feet firmly on the ground.

Top image
HM The Queen WI is welcomed to the WI Life and Leisure Exhibition at Olympia by NFWI Chair Anne Harris, 1984

Bottom image
HRH The Prince of Wales at the WI market stall at the Royal Show, 1978

Moules Marinière

By the mid 1970s the country was still reeling from the impact of the three-day week and yet another recession. January 1976 found Rosemary Wadey encouraging her readers to try the 'cheaper range of fish' to tempt those 'who are not great fish addicts'. Whether cider herrings (costed out at 65p) and fried whiting with orange sauce (74p) would do the trick seems debatable, but this classic French mussel dish, which at 78p was the most expensive dish of the quartet of recipes, is the clear winner here for the more adventurous cook – though how many families sit down together to eat mussels even today is an interesting question.

Serves 4 · Preparation 10 minutes · Cook 20 minutes

2kg mussels
15g butter
1 large onion, peeled and finely chopped
2 cloves garlic, crushed
150ml dry white wine
2 tbsp freshly chopped flat-leaved parsley
salt and freshly ground black pepper

1 Thoroughly scrub the mussels and rinse in cold water until there is no trace of sand left in the water. Discard any that do not close again when given a sharp tap.

2 Melt the butter in a large saucepan, add the onion and garlic and cook gently for several minutes until soft but not coloured. Add wine and seasoning and bring to the boil. Add the mussels, cover pan and simmer gently for 3–4 minutes, shaking the pan frequently and giving a good stir once or twice, until the mussels open up.

3 Add the parsley. Serve the mussels in large soup bowls with the liquid in the bottom, and with plenty of crusty bread.

Home & Country
1976

Economic moules marinière

2½–3 quarts mussels, ½ oz. butter or margarine, 1 large onion, peeled and finely chopped, 2 cloves garlic, crushed (optional), ¼ pint white cooking wine, ½ pint chicken stock (using a cube), salt and pepper, 2 tablespoonfuls freshly chopped parsley, 2 level teaspoonfuls cornflour

Thoroughly scrub mussels and rinse in cold water until there is no trace of sand left in the water. Discard any open mussels which will not close again when given a sharp tap. Melt butter in a large saucepan and fry onion and garlic gently until soft but not coloured. Add wine, stock and salt and pepper and bring to the boil. Cover and simmer gently for 5 minutes. Stir in parsley then add mussels. Cover pan and simmer gently for about 5 minutes. Shake the pan frequently and give a good stir once or twice to make sure mussels are well mixed and open up. Blend cornflour with a little cold water, add to pan and simmer for 2 minutes before serving. Serve mussels in large soup bowls with the liquid in the bottom – this is eaten as a soup after the mussels. Serve with plenty of crusty bread and butter. Serves 4. Approx cost: 78p.

Roast Goose

For plenty of people, life in the country carried on regardless of the fast changing world of the towns and cities. And for many WI members, a goose made a good choice for the Christmas meal. For today's cooks who care about the provenance of their food, goose is an ideal free-range option. Game is also being re-evaluated: it's seasonal, free-range, often very local, low in fat, high in nutrients and easier to cook than many might think. And once again even squirrel (grey, of course) is being promoted as a potential food source for the more adventurous...

Serve 8 · Preparation 10 minutes · Cook 2½ hours

4kg oven-ready goose
1 lemon
2 sprigs fresh rosemary
2–3 tbsp plain flour
salt and freshly ground black
   pepper

1   Follow the method in the original recipe below, stuffing the goose with the lemon, rosemary and salt and pepper, sprinkling it with flour, then roasting it at 200°C/fan oven 180°C/gas mark 6 for the first 20 minutes. Reduce the oven temperature to 180°C/fan oven 160°C/gas mark 4 and roast for a further 2½ hours (or 15 minutes per 500g plus 30 minutes), pouring off the fat from the tin every 30 minutes (use for roast potatoes). Leave to rest for 15–20 minutes before carving.

The WI Poultry and Game Cookbook 1976

Roast Goose

Two ideas were uppermost in writing this book. The first was to make a really good and varied collection of recipes which would help people to make the most of the tremendously increased production in this country of all kinds of poultry, particularly small chickens of the 'broiler' type. The second was to remind our readers how many good ways there are of cooking game. Changes in methods of farming and in the social structure of the country have had an adverse effect on some kinds of game and others, such as quail and ptarmigan (south of the Tweed), for which there were once recipes in every standard cookery book, are now protected by law.

Mature geese weigh from 10–14 lb. Like ducks, they are wasteful so allow 1–1¼ lb per person. A 10 lb goose should feed 8 people. The inside of the goose may be stuffed with either a herb, sage or apple stuffing or it may be rubbed over with lemon and peeled lemon placed inside (to absorb some of the fat) instead of stuffing.

Sprinkle the goose with flour and roast at 400F for 20 minutes. Then lower the heat to 350F and continue cooking. Allow 15 minutes to the lb (a 10 lb goose should take about 2½ hours to cook) but if there is reason to think the goose is on the old and tough side, give it 20 minutes to the lb and 20 over and cook more gently.

Apple sauce is usually served with goose, but all fruit goes well with it. Fried apple or pineapple rings make a good garnish and the gravy is improved if a sour apple is cooked in the pan with the goose.

Cornish Beef Pie

The trying social conditions of the mid to late 1970s saw inflation hit 24.5 per cent in 1975, and hover around the mid teens until 1981. The impact of this state of affairs was felt across the WI membership as women struggled to feed families on wages capped below inflation. Rosemary Wadey's recipes for a feature on feeding a family using that old faithful, beef mince, were designed to make the mince 'stretch for miles, with ample for second helpings... to fill up your family without emptying your purse'. Though feeding a family of six on just one pound of mince seems unlikely to have satisfied hungry tummies...

Serves 6 · Preparation 20 minutes · Cook 45 minutes

500g minced beef
2 medium potatoes, peeled
 and diced
1 large carrot, chopped
1 large onion, finely chopped
1 tbsp chopped fresh thyme
1–2 tbsp Worcestershire sauce
salt and freshly ground black
 pepper
350g ready-made shortcrust
 pastry (choose one made with
 butter for preference)
milk or beaten egg, to glaze

1 Preheat the oven to 210°C/fan oven 190°C/gas mark 7. Combine the mince, potato, carrot, onion, herbs and Worcestershire sauce in a large mixing bowl and season well.

2 Roll out two thirds of the pastry on a floured surface to a rectangle 5cm larger than your tin. Use to line the base and sides of a 28 x 18 x 4cm rectangular baking tin, leaving the edges hanging over the sides. Brush edges with water.

3 Spoon the meat mixture into the pastry and spread evenly. Roll out the remaining pastry to an oblong slightly larger than the tin. Use to cover the meat and press the edges firmly together. Trim off surplus pastry and crimp the edges. Decorate the top with the re-rolled pastry trimmings.

4 Brush the pastry with milk or beaten egg and cook for 20–25 minutes until beginning to brown then reduce the oven temperature to 180°C/fan oven 160°C/gas mark 4 for a further 20 minutes, until the pastry is crisp and golden and the filling cooked through. Serve hot or cold.

Cornish Beef Pie *Serves 6. Approx cost 63p*

1 lb raw minced beef, 1 medium potato, peeled and finely chopped, 1 large carrot, peeled and finely chopped, 1 large onion, peeled and finely chopped, 1 teaspoon dried oregano or thyme, salt and pepper, 12 oz shortcrust pastry (12 oz plain flour, etc), milk or beaten egg to glaze

Mix together the mince, potato, carrot, onion, herbs and plenty of seasoning. Rollout 2/3 pastry and line an oblong tin approx 11 in x 7 in x 3 in. Lay the meat in the pastry and press down evenly. Cover with a lid from the remaining pastry, damp the edges and press firmly together. Trim off surplus pasty and crimp edges. Decorate top with pastry trimmings. Brush with milk or beaten egg and cook at 425F (mark 7) for 20–25 minutes until beginning to brown then reduce to 350F (gas 4) for a further 20 minutes. Serve hot or cold. Serves 6. Approx cost 63p.

Home & Country
1976

Rhubarb and Ginger Jam

The seventies saw the publication of a new series of practical WI books under the WI Home Skills label, overseen as all their cookery books were – and are – by trained professional staff, in this case Pat Cherry, who was then the NFWI's home economics advisor. As the back cover states, these were 'practical guides produced by Britain's unchallenged experts in the field, the National Federation of Women's Institutes'. Other titles included staple skills such as Basketry, Upholstery, Home Wine Making, Dinner Parties and, of course, Patchwork and Quilting.

This classic jam recipe was made with dried root ginger as fresh was not widely available at the time. Our updated recipe comes from The WI Book of Preserves (2008 by Carol Tennant). Don't be tempted to use jam sugar instead of granulated; rhubarb is high in natural pectin so doesn't need a specialist jam sugar.

**Makes 4 x 225g jars · Preparation 20 minutes, plus macerating
Cook 30–50 minutes**

1kg rhubarb, trimmed
1kg granulated sugar
50g preserved stem ginger,
   drained and finely chopped
juice of 1 lemon

1 Cut the rhubarb into 2.5cm pieces. Place in a large bowl, toss with the sugar, cover with a clean tea towel and leave overnight.

2 Next day, pour the rhubarb mixture into a large pan with all its liquid and add the preserved ginger and lemon juice. Bring slowly to the boil, stirring occasionally, until any remaining sugar has dissolved.

3 Boil rapidly for 30 minutes then test for a set. If necessary, boil for a further 5 minutes then test again. Continue until the jam has reached setting point.

4 Remove the pan from the heat, skim off scum and leave to cool for 5 minutes. Pour into sterilised jars, seal and allow to cool before labelling and storing in a cool, dark place.

Rhubarb and Ginger Jam

*Remove leaves and stalks of the rhubarb before weighing it.
Makes approx 2.5 kg (5 lb)*

1.5 kg (3 lb) rhubarb, 1.5 kg (3 lb) sugar, juice of 3 lemons, 25 g (1 oz) dried root ginger

Wash the rhubarb and cut into chunks. Layer these with the sugar in a large bowl. Pour the lemon juice on top and leave to stand overnight. The next day, tip the contents of the bowl into a pan. Bruise the ginger with a hammer and tie it in muslin. Add to the pan. Bring to the boil and boil hard until setting point is reached. Pot into warm jars and cover.

Picnic Fondue

In 1977, we watched open mouthed as Roger Moore supposedly escaped a Soviet ambush on the ski slopes of Austria in the spectacular opening sequence of The Spy Who Loved Me. Glamorous folk of the period headed off to the slopes and came home talking of local dishes of melted cheese. Sales of fondue sets soared.

Another favourite of the decade, especially with the men, was the barbeque and the adventurous cook of the late seventies was encouraged to add more interest to the outdoor cooking experience. She could try a pizza cooked in a frying pan over the coals, or how about her favourite recipe for cheese fondue? What's more, this one could be cooked on a portable gas stove 'if you do not want to launch yourself headfirst into the barbecue scene'! As regards types of cheese, witness how far we have come in 35 years – the range of high-quality regional cheeses, especially British ones made by small specialist producers, improves all the time.

Serves 4 · Preparation 15 minutes · Cook 15 minutes

1 clove garlic, peeled and halved
300ml dry cider or white wine
2 tsp French mustard
50g blue cheese such as Stilton, crumbled
225g Emmental or Beaufort cheese, grated
225g strong Cheddar, grated
1 tbsp cornflour
50ml kirsch (optional)
salt and pepper
cubed crusty white bread, to serve

1 Rub the inside of a medium heavy-based pan with the cut side of the garlic. Heat the cider, mustard and seasoning in the pan until simmering.

2 Stir in the blue cheese and continue cooking until it has melted. Stir in the remainder of the cheese and heat gently till melted but do not boil. Mix the cornflour with the kirsch or a little water and stir it into the melted cheese. Cook gently until the mixture is thick and creamy. Serve with bread and fondue forks for dipping.

Picnic Fondue

Eat this at once by spearing chunks of French bread on forks and dunking in the pan. 300 ml (½ pint) cider, 2 x 5 ml spoons (2 teaspoons) French mustard. 50 g (2 oz), Danish blue cheese,225 g (8 oz) Dutch cheese, 225 g (8 oz) soft Cheddar cheese, 1 x 15 ml spoon (1 tablespoon) cornflour, garlic (optional), salt and pepper

Heat the cider, mustard, salt and pepper in a heavy pan. Grate all the cheeses. Stir in the blue cheese and continue cooking until it has melted. Remove the pan from the heat and stir in the remainder of the cheese. Slake the cornflour with a little water and stir it in. Cook gently until the mixture is thick and creamy.

Cream of Broad Bean Soup

The seventies was the era of the dinner party. One of the WI Home Skills' series of books, Dinner Parties promised recipes that would 'help you eat your way around the calendar'. As Mrs Cozens of the WI points out on the opening page: 'Like the weather, dishes have seasons'. Shops and supermarkets were increasingly full of imported products and consumers were becoming used to luxuries such as strawberries all year round – though even then it was felt these interlopers didn't taste as good as the seasonal British strawberry. As part of Summer Menu No.2 Broad Bean Soup was advised, as if the weather was cold it could be served hot!

Serves 8 · Preparation 15 minutes · Cook 20 minutes

WI Home Skills:
Dinner Parties
1979

Broad bean soup

700g (1½ lb) shelled broad beans, sprig of savory or thyme, 1 small onion, 50 g (2 oz) butter, 35g (1½ oz) flour, 2 litres (3 pints) stock, 8 x 15ml spoons (8 tablespoons) double cream, chopped parsley or chervil, salt and pepper

Cook the beans in boiling salted water (just enough to cover) with the savory or thyme. Drain and reserve the liquid. Refresh the beans under the cold tap and drain well again.

Meanwhile, peel and chop the onion finely. Fry in melted butter until soft. Stir in the flour and cook for another 2–3 minutes. Add the stock and bring to the boil. Season to taste and simmer for 10 minutes.

Reserve a few beans for garnish and add the rest to the soup. Simmer for a few minutes, then pass through a vegetable mill.

Just before serving, remove the outer skins from the reserved beans and add, with some of the cooking liquor to the soup. Mix the cream and parsley or chervil together in a bowl. Bring the soup back to the boil and pour a little on to the cream mixture. Stir well, tip back into the pan and reheat gently. Adjust seasoning and serve.

Cooking this recipe today...
Follow the original recipe but don't salt the cooking water for the beans. Drain it off and use it to make up the stock to 2 litres. Omit the cream and parsley or chervil for a lighter soup.

Brandy Snaps

For mothers organising a children's party, the main work was all in the cooking. The author of WI Home Skills: Picnics, Barbecues and Children's Parties *expects her reader to work hard. Although her advice was to 'keep it simple and as non-messy as possible', the menus are elaborate compared to today's offerings. How many of us would make brandy snaps from scratch? She goes on, 'the important factor is to keep everything small and... colourful on the table'. And it seems ice cream should be served towards the end of the party but, maybe surprisingly 'jelly is not very popular with any age group and is best therefore omitted'!*

Preparation 30 minutes · Cook 30–40 minutes

Brandy Snaps

100 g (4 oz) flour, 1 x 5ml spoon (1 teaspoon) ground ginger, 100 g (4 oz) sugar, 100 g (4 oz) butter, 100 g (4 oz) golden syrup, juice of 1 lemon, whipped cream

Sift the flour and ginger together and warm in an oven. Sift again. Melt the sugar, butter and syrup together and add the lemon juice. Stir in the warmed flour. Put small spoonfuls of the mixture, very well spaced, on to buttered baking sheets and bake for 8-10 minutes at 160-180C, 325-350 F, Gas 3-4. Leave to cool for a few seconds, then remove and roll round a wooden spoon handle. When quite cold and ready to serve, fill with whipped cream, piped from a forcing bag.
Note *Brandy snaps will keep for a few days in a tin, unfilled, but they are very fragile and must be handled with care.*

Cooking this recipe today...
Follow the original recipe, but there is no need to warm the flour and ginger. We recommend reducing the amount of lemon juice to the juice of ½ a lemon. Use baking parchment instead of buttering your baking sheets. And bake the snaps at 180˚C/fan oven 170˚C/ gas mark 4. Do note you won't be able to roll them up if they get too cold but you can always pop them back in the over briefly to soften them up again. We filled them with whipped double cream rather than whipping cream.

Nettle Champ

Writing in the introduction to The Countryside Yearbook, *a WI calendar of seasonal recipes, author Gail Duff promoted the use of 'wild' plants throughout the year. She writes: 'Somehow, with two world wars to cope with, the gradual increase of the convenience food market and the ease with which patent medicines could be obtained, everyone forgot that the countryside yields a wealth of useable plants.' But she was happy to report in 1982, 'two generations later, the tide is turning again'. It's a trend that has gained great pace, over the past decade in particular, as high-end chefs vie with each other to serve up unusual foraged ingredients on their Michelin-starred menus.*

Nettles are one of the most easily sourced, nutritious and tasty of wild plants, best picked in March and April when the fresh growth is tender and at its best. Pick just the tips before they become tough. The yearbook's advice was to 'take a pair of rubber gloves'. Dropping nettles into boiling water, milk or stock gets rid of the sting so you can eat them without fear.

Serves 4–6 · Preparation 15 minutes · Cook 20 minutes

The Countryside Yearbook 1982

Champ

Champ, made with potatoes and nettles, can be served as a side dish or as a light meal in itself. In Ireland, it was once served for the children's supper, accompanied by a glass of buttermilk.

675g (1 ½ lbs) potatoes, 1 small onion, thinly sliced, 50g (2 oz) nettle tops, 275ml (½ pint) milk, 50g (2oz) butter, freshly ground black pepper

Boil the potatoes, in their skins, with the onion until they are soft. Drain them, let them steam dry and skin them. Return them to the saucepan and mash them with the onion.

While the potatoes are cooking, wash and finely chop the nettles. Put them into a saucepan with the milk and boil them for 10 minutes. The milk will curdle but this does not matter. Put the saucepan of potatoes on a low heat and mix in the nettles and milk. Season with the pepper and stir on a low heat for 2 minutes so the puree dries a little. Put the champ either onto one large plate or four small ones. Make a well in the centre and put in the butter. Serves 4.

Cooking this recipe today...
After preparing and cooking the potatoes as above, simmer 200ml milk in a medium pan and add the washed but not chopped nettles. Bring to the boil and cook gently for a minute or two until wilted to remove the sting. Blitz in a liquidiser or with a hand blender before adding to the mashed potatoes with 20 – 30g butter to taste. Beat until smooth and season well.

Spiced Whisky Cake

In 1983 Rosemary Wadey encouraged Home & Country readers to be more adventurous in a feature entitled 'Spice It Up'. She advocated moving on from cinnamon, ginger and mixed spice that most people used every day, but when experimenting with unfamiliar spices cautioned 'add them – sparingly at first – to enhance and lift other flavours in the food, but definitely not to disguise them completely'. This wonderful cake recipe shows just how cautious she was proposing the reader should be – with an audacious ½ teaspoon of ground cloves. But she was, of course, right. Balanced spicing is an art, and too heavy-handed an application can swiftly ruin the subtleties of a dish.

The recipe stands as it is for modern cooks. The metrication has settled into a pattern we are familiar with and the method is easy to follow.

Makes 1 x 20cm sandwich cake · Preparation 30 minutes · Cook 55 minutes

Home & Country
1983

Spiced Whisky Cake

200 g/8 oz sultanas, 150 ml/¼ pint water, 100 g/4 oz butter or margarine, 125 g/5 oz soft brown sugar, 1 large egg, beaten, 150 g/6 oz plain flour, 1 level teaspoon bicarbonate of soda, ½ level teaspoon ground cloves, ¼ level teaspoon ground cinnamon, 75 g/3 oz walnuts or pecan nuts, chopped, 2 tablespoons whisky
Butter cream: 75 g/3 oz butter, 1 egg yolk, 200 g/8 oz icing sugar, sifted, 1 tablespoon whisky, walnut halves or pecan halves for decoration

Grease two 20cm/8 in round deep sandwich tins and line the bases with greased greaseproof paper. Put the sultanas and water into a small pan and bring to the boil. Simmer gently for 15 minutes. Strain off the liquor and make up to 100 ml/4 fl oz with cold water. Leave to cool. Cream the butter or margarine together with the sugar until very pale and fluffy, then beat in the egg. Sift the flour with the soda and spices and fold into the mixture alternating with the sultana liquor. Add the walnuts, sultanas and the whisky, and mix lightly but evenly. Divide between tins and level the tops. Bake in a moderate oven 180C/fan oven 160C/gas mark 4 for 30-40 minutes or until firm. Cool for a few minutes in the tin, then loosen the edges and turn very carefully on to a wire rack to cool.

For the butter cream, melt the butter in a saucepan. Remove from the heat and beat in the egg yolk. Gradually beat in the icing sugar, alternating with the whisky until light, smooth and fluffy. Use one third to sandwich the cakes together and the remainder to spread on the top. Make an attractive design on top using a round bladed knife and decorate with walnuts or pecans.

White Bread

In June 1983 Home & Country celebrated the booming homemade food business. WI markets (the first was started by the Lewes WI in 1919), were expanding their range of homemade produce. A feature announced: 'Whether you bake for pleasure or for profit, or as an annual contributor to the church fete', you may find 'a profitable outlet for culinary talents' by cooking for local markets.

WI markets can be viewed as increasingly successful forerunners of the burgeoning farmers' market movement of the 21st century. In fact, such was their success that in 1990 when the NFWI became a charitable company, the £10 million turnover of the markets clashed with the ethos of the not-for-profit organisation. As a result, in 1995, the markets separated from the NFWI and became self-financing.

Back in 1983 members were encouraged to bake all kinds of cakes 'from fruit to fancy iced'. All shapes and sizes of rolls and loaves were likely to go down well with shoppers too, as people are 'only too glad to buy a real home-made loaf'. This recipe for an enriched white loaf can be followed just as it stands.

Makes 2 loaves · Preparation 30 minutes, plus kneading and proving
Cook 45 minutes

Enriched white bread

WI Book of Bread and Buns 1984

Makes 2 plaits or 12 rolls

450 g/1 lb strong plain white flour, 1 tsp salt, 15 g/ ½ oz fresh yeast or 7 g (¼ oz) dried yeast, 1 tsp sugar, 250 ml (8 fl oz) warm milk, 50 g (2 oz) butter, softened, 1 egg, beaten
Egg wash: *1 egg, 1 tbsp water, 1 tsp sugar*

Weigh out 100g (4 oz) flour and keep on one side. Sift the remaining flour and salt into a bowl. Add the fresh or dried yeast to the sugar, lukewarm milk and reserved flour and mix well to form a batter. Leave to stand for about 20 minutes in a warm place until frothing vigorously. Add to the flour with the butter and beaten egg, and mix well. The dough will be quite soft. Turn onto a lightly floured board and knead for 10 minutes (or 2–3 minutes with a dough hook on an electric mixer). Form into a ball and put into a bowl. Cover and leave to prove for 45 minutes.

Heat the oven to 190C (375F) Mark 5. Knead the dough again and shape into two plaits or 12 rolls. Place on a lightly greased baking sheet. Make the egg wash by beating the egg with the water and sugar. Brush all over the surface of the dough. Cover and prove for 30 minutes. Bake loaves for 45 minutes, or rolls for 15 minutes, until the base sounds hollow when tapped. Cool on a wire rack.

This dough may be flavoured with dried fruit, nuts or grated orange rind, and may be decorated with icing when cold. If fruit is added, the dough will take longer to rise.

Margaret Hanford conducting a cookery demonstration
to WI members at Denman College,
1990

1986–1995

You are what you eat

A decade of momentous change throughout the world witnessed the fall of the Berlin Wall, the release of Nelson Mandela, the first Gulf War and the stock market crash known as Black Monday. At home the recession that began in 1990 saw unemployment reach nearly three million at its peak three years on. A decade of momentous change throughout the world witnessed the stock market crash on Black Monday, the fall of the Berlin Wall, the release of Nelson Mandela and the first Gulf War. At home the recession that began in 1990 saw unemployment reach nearly three million at its peak three years on. In lean times, then as now, we turn to home comforts for reassurance, and the recipes of this period reflect this trend. But at the same time the WI was focusing on events in the wider world. In 1993, two members from South Yorkshire were inspired to start an initiative delivering aid to Romania, which led to a ten-year project to develop a women's group in Tirgu Mures, similar to the WI. Twelve federations were eventually involved teaching a range of workshops including dressmaking, keep fit, and craft amongst many others, and in 1998 the Women's Forum in Mures Country was formed.

This period was also one of transformation at home, as the mechanisation of production that had transformed the British food industry after the war continued to affect the country. Food scares such as Salmonela and BSE had a huge impact on the farming industry and the way we viewed our food producers. The mid eighties saw the first sales of organic foods in supermarkets (and Pat and Tony Archer moved their farm over to organic production in The Archers). In 1982 The Food and Drink Programme, produced by Peter Bazalgette – who would go on to create Ready Steady Cook (1994), Changing Rooms (1996) and Big Brother (2000) – was launched on BBC2. It was the dawn of the move from the home economist (mostly female) to the age of the celebrity chef (mostly male). But what was the average woman in the British countryside cooking in her home, what were her concerns when feeding the family? How was she preparing her children for the world they would enter? The WI continued with its mission to support and educate her.

'The WI crosses all boundaries...The jam and cakes image gives way to an era of politics and caring concern.' 1986 *Today*

Left image
WI members on the steps of the Albert
Memorial at the NFWI AGM, 1986

Right: top image
HM The Queen speaks at the 75th
NFWI AGM, 1990

Right: bottom image
WI's tough call on child abuse during
the NFWI AGM, 1986

Victoria Sandwich

The quintessential British cake, a good Victoria sponge still remains a staple of many WI meetings. Recipes for sponge cakes have appeared in WI publications going back to the earliest days of the movement, and reputations have been made and destroyed with cakes such as this one. The WI rules when judging are precise: only raspberry jam for the filling; a dusting of caster, NEVER icing, sugar to finish, and a 20cm (8 in) diameter. Good flavour should be at the heart of the cake's success, so use finest quality butter and fresh free-range eggs – if you have your own hens, even better. The debate on what makes a perfect Victoria still rages on: butter or margarine, or a mix of both; to sift or double sift the flour; to add vanilla; is it a sandwich or a sponge? The simple format of this recipe shows just how assured WI cooks must have been. A WI recipe featured on the Hairy Bikers' BBC2 show in 2011, and our updated recipe is based on that one (which you can also find on the WI website).

Serves 4 · Makes one 20cm cake · Cook 25–30 minutes

3 medium free-range eggs, weighed in their shells (around 170g)
the weight of the eggs in softened butter or soft margarine, caster sugar and self-raising flour
homemade or good-quality shop-bought raspberry jam, to fill

1 Preheat the oven to 180°C/fan oven 160°C/gas mark 4. Grease and base-line two 20cm sandwich tins with baking parchment.

2 Cream the butter/margarine and sugar together until very pale and fluffy. Beat the eggs then gradually add to the mixture a tablespoonful at a time, beating well.

3 Sift the flour and gently fold into the mixture with a metal spoon. Divide the mixture equally between the prepared tins and level the surface, making a slight hollow in the centre to allow the cakes to rise.

4 Bake for 25–30 minutes on the same shelf in the oven until well risen and golden. The cakes should have shrunk from the sides of the tin and spring back when touched.

5 Remove the cakes from the tins and turn onto a wire rack to cool. When cold, sandwich them together with jam and dust with caster sugar.

Devon WI Cookery Book 1987

Victoria sponge

4 ozs. sugar, 4 ozs. margarine, 4 ozs. self-raising flour, 2 eggs.

Cream together for 15 minutes. Add alternately to above, sifted flour and eggs.

Bake in oven 365F, 185C, Gas Mark 4.

Crème Caramel

In 1987 the Devon Federation produced a revised edition of their cookbook to reflect the 'many changes in eating habits and methods of cooking', including vegetarian and microwave recipes. By 1986 a quarter of American households owned a domestic microwave oven and their rising popularity here saw a rush of microwave cookery books, with recipes for everything from meringues to Christmas dinner. But the variation in oven types and the need to stop, stir and re-cover food made cooking in them a chore. Nowadays we do very little 'scratch' cooking in microwaves. And testing this recipe reminded us why. Both the caramel and custard overcooked in seconds. So our updated recipe is done the traditional way.

Serves 6 · Preparation 20 minutes · Cook 30 minutes, and chill overnight

115g granulated sugar
40g caster sugar
3 medium free-range eggs
450ml full-fat milk

Crème Caramel

Caramel: 2 tablespoons granulated sugar,
2 tablespoons water
Egg custard: ½ pint milk,
1 tablespoon sugar, 2 eggs

Caramel: Stir the sugar and water in a heatproof jug and microwave on HIGH, stirring once, until sugar is dissolved. Caramelize the sugar syrup by bringing to the boil. Cook 3–4 minutes. Inspect every half-minute as the syrup burns quickly. Pour into the base of a 1-pint ovenproof soufflé dish.
Custard: Beat the eggs and sugar, add the milk. Beat well and strain over the caramel. Cook, turning once, approximately 3½–4 minutes.

1 Preheat the oven to 160°C/fan oven 140°C/gas mark 2. Mix the granulated sugar with 4½ tablespoons cold water in a heavy-based pan and heat gently until dissolved. Don't let the sugar boil before it's dissolved or it will start to crystallise. Bring to the boil and cook over a high heat for a couple of minutes without stirring until a rich golden brown, checking constantly so that the syrup doesn't burn. Pour it into the base of a 725ml deep ovenproof dish (a soufflé dish is ideal) or six individual 125ml ramekins, and tip to coat the base in the caramel.

2 For the custard, beat the caster sugar and eggs together then whisk in the milk. Strain the custard over the caramel. Place the dish or ramekins in a roasting tin filled with warm water and bake for 25–30 minutes until the custard is just starting to set. There should be no bubbles on the surface – a sign that the custard has curdled. Leave to cool then chill overnight.

3 To serve, loosen the custard around the edge with a small palette knife then turn out onto a serving dish.

Note: Be very careful when preparing the caramel as sugar syrup is very hot.

Herb Baked Chicken

Since its inception the WI has been concerned with the health of the nation. The importance of good nutrition has always been highlighted, alongside good flavour and ethically produced ingredients, from the earliest days. The introduction to the WI Book of Healthy Family Cookery, quotes British physiologist and nutritionist Professor John Yudkin, famous for his views on sugar consumption: 'You are what you eat'. It goes on to say that 'in order to be fit and well and enjoy a sense of vitality, it is essential to eat a balanced diet as well as taking plenty of exercise and getting an adequate amount of sleep'. As ever the WI provides a calm clear voice of common sense in times of confusion.

This recipe uses herbs for an intense, satisfying and healthy burst of flavour.

Serves 4 · Preparation 10 minutes · Cook 30 minutes

Herb Baked Chicken

The WI Book of Healthy Family Cookery 1989

Serves 4
Salt and freshly ground black pepper, 4 chicken breasts, 1 tbsp sunflower oil, 2 medium onions, grated rind and juice of 1 large lemon, 4 tbsp chopped fresh parsley, 1 tbsp chopped fresh thyme, 1 tbsp chopped fresh rosemary, 1 tbsp chopped fresh mint, 150 ml (¼ pint) stock

Heat the oven to 180C (350F) gas mark 4. Season and brush the breasts with the oil and bake uncovered for 30 minutes. Finely chop the onions and place in a bowl with the lemon rind and juice. Add the herbs and mix well. Season to taste.
Remove the chicken from the oven and pour off any surplus fat. Pour the stock over the chicken. Press the onion and herb mixture on top of the chicken breasts and bake for 15-20 minutes until the herb topping is crisp and lightly browned. Serve hot or cold.

Cooking this recipe today...
Chicken breasts came on the bone in those days – so choose chicken thighs on the bone or chicken breast fillets and cook for 25–30 minutes in total, adding the topping halfway through. You can leave the skin on (as would have been the case with the original) or remove it to reduce fat content. And use one red onion for a more subtle flavour. Serve with a salad and steamed new potatoes.

Avocado Pear Vinaigrette

The WI Book of Healthy Family Cookery *sheds a fascinating light on some of the key issues still facing modern cooks today. One is the concern with 'use by' and 'best before' dates. The reader is warned: 'It is still possible to buy really fresh fruit and vegetables from self-service supermarkets, or from market stalls... rather than those sold under hot lights in some of the supermarkets.' Avocados are a case in point – you really need to feel them to test for ripeness and they are one instance where 'use by' dates are useless. Make sure that they are perfectly ripe when trying the recipe for this classic salad.*

'Sell by' and 'use by' dates have exerted something of a tyranny at the cost of common sense and we now throw away up to a third of all foods purchased. This issue was revisited by WI members via The WI Great Food Debates in 2013, where reducing food waste was highlighted as a key way of ensuring future food security.

Serves 4 · Preparation 10 minutes

The WI Book of
Healthy Family Cookery
1989

Avocado Pear Vinaigrette

Serves 4

2 large firm ripe avocado pears, 2 tbsp lemon juice, vinaigrette dressing, watercress sprigs, salt and pepper
For the vinaigrette dressing: *2–3 tbsp corn or groundnut oil, pinch of dry mustard, salt and black pepper, 1 tbsp white wine vinegar, ½ tsp chopped chives, ½ tsp chopped parsley, ½ tsp chopped fresh dill, tarragon or chervil, 1 tsp finely chopped capers, 1 tsp finely chopped pitted green olives or gherkin*

Halve the pears lengthways and remove the stones. The flesh should not be discoloured or soft (see below). Brush the cut surfaces with lemon juice at once. Place a half pear, cut side up, on each of four small plates. Fill the hollows with vinaigrette sauce, and garnish the plates with watercress.

If the pears are discoloured or soft when cut open, take out the good quality flesh in slivers, toss it with dressing and mix with cubed fresh or canned fruit (not bananas) or with salad vegetables. Serve in dessert glasses or bowls as a "cocktail".

For the vinaigrette, mix the oil and seasonings and stir or beat in the vinegar drop by drop until an emulsion forms. Add the flavourings, mix well, and leave to stand for 1–2 hours before use.

Cooking this recipe today...

The only updating this recipe needs is to substitute 3 tablespoons of olive oil for corn oil in the dressing and increase the herbs to a tablespoon of each. Garnishing the plate with watercress will give it a lovely retro touch but you can omit it happily.

Tiffin

Favourite Tastes from Worcestershire *was produced as part of the celebrations for the 75th anniversary of the Worcestershire Federation. It opened with a page of sensible microwave tips that still stand up well today: advice on how to restore honey, how to dry fresh herbs and, one of the oven's most useful functions for the cook, melting chocolate. Although two minutes per 100g of chocolate might have done the trick with the lower-powered ovens of the period, if attempted in today's more high-spec versions, using the top-quality chocolate we have become accustomed to, it would certainly cause problems with 'seizing'.*

Back then, low-grade chocolate or substitutes were recommended for cooking – note that this recipe for Tiffin specifies 'cooking chocolate'. But just like cooking with wine, the better the quality, the better the results. Today's booming demand for specialist chocolate and the recognised benefits of dark chocolate as a 'super food' has transformed the industry in the 21st century.

Makes 16 · Preparation 15 minutes

Favourite Tastes from Worcestershire 1992

Tiffin

4 ozs (100g) margarine, 8 ozs (225g) cooking chocolate, 8 ozs (225g) Rich Tea biscuits, crushed, 2 tablespoons (2x15ml) syrup, 1 tablespoon (15ml) caster sugar, 4 ozs (100g) raisins, 2 dessertspoonfuls (3x10ml) drinking chocolate

Method: *Melt together the margarine, sugar, syrup and drinking chocolate. Add the raisins and biscuits. Mix well.*

Spread the mixture in a Swiss roll tin and run melted cooking chocolate on top. Cut into small pieces when cold.

Great favourite with children (and adults) and on a cake stall.
Brenda Owen, Hollywood WI

Cooking this recipe today...
Simply follow the recipe as given but use good-quality milk or dark chocolate for the best results. A Swiss roll tin measures 32 x 22 x 4cm.

Banana and Date Chutney

In January 1993 Home & Country *magazine ran a feature on cooking with bananas, at the time the best-selling fruit in the country. In 1992 the WI became a founder member of the Fairtrade Foundation. The Fairtrade Certification Mark appeared initially on tea and coffee and is now applied to more than 4,500 products from bananas to cotton, and even gold.*

Rosemary Wadey recommended using firm bananas for cooking and suggested serving this chutney with ploughman's lunches. Her recipe came sandwiched between two other pieces of editorial. The first asked for members to participate in a national survey on how easy it was to find healthier food in shops. And the second was a news page featuring a flurry of correspondence on the singing of Jerusalem at meetings. Nowadays many WIs have dropped the practice but Jerusalem is still sung at Federation annual conferences and swells the space in the Albert Hall for the AGM.

Makes approx 1.1kg · Preparation 20 minutes · Cook 1½–2 hours

450g onions, finely chopped
225g stoned dates, finely chopped
1kg ripe bananas, peeled and sliced
600ml pickling vinegar or cider vinegar
50g black treacle
225g light brown sugar
2 tsp ground ginger
1 tsp ground allspice
grated rind of 1 lemon
2 cloves garlic, crushed
½ tsp salt

1 Place the onions and dates in a medium heavy-based saucepan. Add the bananas to the pan with the vinegar. Bring slowly to the boil and cook gently together for about 30 minutes, stirring occasionally until tender.

2 Add the treacle, sugar, ginger, allspice, lemon rind, garlic and salt and continue to simmer, uncovered, for 1–1½ hours stirring occasionally until thick and dark brown in colour – you should be able to run a spoon across the base of the pan and it will leave a channel.

3 Remove the pan from the heat and leave to stand for 5 minutes. Pour into sterilised jars, seal, and allow to cool before labelling and storing in a cool, dark place. Store for 2–3 weeks before use.

Home & Country
1993

Banana and date chutney *Makes approx 1.1 kg (2½ lb)*

450g/1lb onions, peeled, 225g/8oz stoned dates, 6-8 bananas (approx 900g/2lb), 600ml/1pint pickling vinegar, 100g/4oz black treacle, 225g/8oz brown sugar, 2 level teaspoons ground ginger, 1 level teaspoon ground allspice, grated rind of 1-2 lemons, 1 level teaspoon salt, 2 cloves garlic, crushed

Finely chop or mince the onions and dates and put into a saucepan. Peel and slice the bananas and add to the pan with the vinegar. Bring slowly back to the boil and cook gently until tender. Add the rest of the ingredients and continue to simmer, uncovered, until thick and dark brown. Stir to prevent sticking. Pot and cover in the usual way, and store for 2-3 weeks before use.

Beef Wellington

A step by step guide to making your own puff pastry from Rosemary Wadey was the centrepiece of a recipe for the classic Beef Wellington in 1993. But the WI was moving with the times and accepted that though some members might make their own pastry from scratch, many others had neither the skill or the time to do so. As Rosemary says, 'making your own isn't a quick process... but well worth the effort. If time is at a premium or you can't face making your own, there are some very good alternatives available'. All kinds of convenience foods were appearing in supermarkets offering short cuts and labour saving for busy women and good quality ready-made puff pastry, frozen or chilled, put this dish within the reach of everyday cooks. Now we go one step better and have access to excellent quality ready-made pastries made with butter rather than vegetable fat, as in the original home made version.

Serves 6 · Preparation 30 minutes · Cook 1 hour

Beef Wellington

This must be one of the favourite 'en croute' dishes of all time. Fillet steak is not cheap but there is no wastage, and this makes an excellent dish for a celebration.

2 tablespoons oil, 675g/1 ½ lb piece of fillet of beef (thick end), 2 onions, peeled and finely chopped, 100 g/4 oz mushrooms, chopped, 2 level tablespoons chopped fresh parsley, 1 level teaspoonful chopped fresh thyme, 1-2 cloves garlic, crushed, 3-4 tablespoons freshly made breadcrumbs, salt and pepper, 450 g/1 lb puff pastry
Beaten egg to glaze

Heat the oil in a pan and fry the fillet of beef on all sides until well sealed and lightly browned – about 8 minutes. Remove from the heat and leave to cool. Fry the onions in the same fat until soft and lightly coloured, add the mushrooms and continue cooking for a few minutes more. Remove from the heat and mix in the herbs, garlic, breadcrumbs and plenty of seasoning. Allow to cool. Roll out the pastry to a rectangle large enough to enclose the beef. Spread the mushroom mixture over the pastry and place the beef on top. Wrap the beef completely in the pastry, damping the edges to seal, then place on a greased baking sheet with the seam underneath and the ends tucked under. Decorate the top with a double row of leaves made from the pastry trimmings. Glaze well and make one or two small slits. Bake in a hot oven (220C/425F/Gas mark 7) for about 40 minutes until the pastry is well puffed and browned. At this stage the beef should be rare. If more cooking is required lower the temperature to moderate (180C/350F/Gas mark 4) and cook for a further 15 minutes for medium to well done. Serve hot or cold. Serve 6.

Cooking this recipe today...
Make the Beef Wellington using a 500g block ready-made puff pastry made with butter, defrosted if frozen. Use chestnut mushrooms for the best flavour, and medium onions. We prefer our meat rarer so reduce cooking times to 25-30 minutes in the oven for medium rare.

Fricassée of Rabbit with Apples

1993 saw the return to the television screens of WI member Ruth Mott, with gardener Harry Dodson, in an evocative sequel to their popular The Victorian Kitchen Garden series. BBC Two's The Wartime Kitchen and Garden looked back at the Dig for Victory campaign and wartime recipes such as Woolton Pie, created in 1940 by the chef of London's Savoy hotel to use up leftover vegetables. After all the furore and insecurity over food scares such as BSE, this nostalgia for what were seen as simpler times extended into our kitchens. The recipe book accompanying the series was well received, and Ruth's reputation led to her acting as a historic food consultant to the film Gosford Park.

Rabbit recipes had been a mainstay of Home & Country since its early issues and as Rosemary Wadey said in the introduction to this dish, 'rabbit dishes are becoming more popular again now that this versatile low fat meat is more widely available, fresh or frozen'.

Serves 3–4 · Preparation 25 minutes · Cook 45 minutes

Home & Country
1993

Fricassée of Rabbit with Apples

1 rabbit, prepared and jointed, 2-3 level tablespoons flour, 50g/2oz butter or margarine, 4 rashers streaky bacon, 1 large onion, peeled and sliced, 2-3 sticks celery, sliced, 2 Bramley apples, peeled and sliced, 275ml/½ pint milk, approx 450ml/ ¾ pint chicken stock, 1 bay leaf, ½ level teaspoon dried rosemary, crumbled, salt and pepper, lemon juice, celery leaves to garnish

Coat the rabbit joints in the flour and fry in hot fat in a flameproof casserole until browned all over. Remove. Fry the bacon, onion and celery in the same fat until soft but not coloured, add the apples and continue to fry for a little longer. Stir in enough flour to absorb the fat, then gradually blend in the milk and bring to the boil. Put the rabbit back in the casserole then add sufficient stock to barely cover the joints. Add the herbs, plenty of seasoning and a teaspoon or two of lemon juice to taste. Bring back to the boil, cover and cook in a moderate oven (180C/350F/Gas Mark 4) for 45-60 minutes or until tender. If the sauce is too thin put into a saucepan and boil hard until reduced a little. Adjust the seasoning and pour back over the rabbit. Garnish with celery leaves. Serves 4-5.

Cooking this recipe today...

Ask your butcher or game dealer to joint the rabbit for you or buy it already jointed from the supermarket. Simply replace the dried rosemary with 1 tbsp of chopped fresh leaves and replace half of the stock with white wine or cider and cook as directed with the oven set at 160°C/ fan oven 150°C/ gas mark 3 for 40–45 minutes. Given today's appetites, we think this recipe serves 3-4 rather than 4-5.

Green Vegetable Curry

In 1995, recipes from the WI Book of... *series were brought together in one volume,* The Women's Institute Book of Home Cooking. *The WI was trying to move with the times. 'In keeping with today's attitudes towards eating' this compendium marks a 'shift from recipes with lashings of wine and double cream' to 'good fresh food, simply prepared with the minimum of added fat'. This healthy vegetable curry recipe is still rather old fashioned by today's standards, with its reconstituted desiccated coconut.*

Serves 4 · Preparation 20 minutes · Cook 25 minutes

2 tbsp sunflower oil
2 medium onions, finely chopped
2 cloves garlic, finely chopped
2 tbsp medium curry paste (or use individual spices as in the original recipe)
½ green cabbage, shredded
150g peas, defrosted if frozen
150g green beans, thickly sliced
250g potatoes, peeled and cubed
400g can coconut milk
1 tbsp lemon juice
salt
chopped fresh coriander, to garnish

1   Heat the oil in a medium heavy-based pan, add the onions and stir until lightly browned. Add the garlic and curry paste and stir for another couple of minutes. Add the prepared vegetables to the pan, season with salt and cook for 3–4 minutes, stirring once or twice to coat in the spices.

2   Add the coconut milk and lemon juice to the pan and bring to the boil. Simmer gently for 10–15 minutes until the vegetables are tender. Check seasoning, add the chopped coriander and serve with steamed brown rice.

Green Vegetable Curry
Serves 4–6
100 g (4 oz) desiccated coconut, 2 tsp ground coriander, 1¼ tsp each ground cumin and ginger, pinch each ground cinnamon and cloves, 1/3 tsp chilli powder, 1/3 tsp turmeric, 75 g (3 oz) shredded cabbage, 100 g (4 oz) green peas, shelled, 100g (4 oz) green beans, sliced, 225 g (8 oz) potatoes, peeled and diced, 3 tbsp corn oil, 2 medium sized onions, chopped, 50 g (2 oz) green pepper, deseeded and chopped, ¼–½ tsp salt, 2 tsp lemon juice

Make the coconut milk and spice mixed well ahead. Pour 275 ml (½ pint) boiling water over the desiccated coconut. Leave for 2 hours. Process with the liquid in a blender then strain through a cloth-lined sieve and squeeze out all the milk. Mix all the spices together and set aside. Put the cabbage, peas, beans and potatoes in 275 ml (½ pint) boiling water in a pan. Simmer for 5 minutes and drain. Heat the oil in a second pan, add onions and stir until browned. Add the pepper and spices and stir. Add the vegetables, season and cook for 4 minutes, stirring once or twice. Add the coconut milk and lemon juice and cook gently until the vegetables are tender.

The Women's Institute Book of Home Cooking 1995

Pavlova

'Meringues are everyone's favourites', so says the introduction to the meringue section of The Women's Institute Book of Home Cooking. *And it's as true today – we still love the crisp outside and soft gooey centre of a classic Pavlova. And if you follow the rules for good meringue it's one of the simplest desserts to make. There is a rather odd twist to this particular recipe – it's cooked in a dish and served warm. We've suggested a more typical chilled variation when cooking this recipe today.*

Serves 6 · Preparation 30 minutes · Cook 1 hour

Pavlova

Serves 6–8

whites of medium 4 eggs, 175 g (6 oz) caster sugar, 4 tsp cornflour, 2 tsp white wine vinegar, 275 ml (½ pint) whipping cream, 4 fresh peaches

Heat the oven to 120C (250F) mark ½.
Whisk the egg whites until stiff. Add the sugar, 2 tablespoons at a time, beating between each addition. When the sugar is used up, beat for 1-2 minutes until the meringue is dense, velvety and very, very stiff. Then beat in the cornflour, sprinkling it over the meringue, and finally the vinegar.
Butter an attractive shallow ovenproof dish. Put the meringue into it, making a hollow dip in the centre. Bake for 1½ hours until really firm and set.
Whip the cream. Peel and slice the peaches and fold into the cream. When the meringue is cooked, put the fruit into it. Serve without too much delay.

Cooking this recipe today...
This recipe needs little adaptation. To serve the Pavlova cold, line a baking sheet with baking parchment and draw a 20cm circle on it. Spoon the meringue into the circle and spread it out to fill it. Make a hollow in the centre. Bake for 1 hour until the outside is crisp but the centre soft. Turn off the oven and leave the meringue to cool inside it. It may sink and crack a little but that is part of its charm. Use 400–500g soft summer fruit for the filling.

Prime Minister Tony Blair addressing the NFWI Triennial
General Meeting with NFWI Chair Helen Carey

1996–2005

Into the new millennium

Chair Helen Carey welcomed the new century with the statement that the 'Women's Institute is needed today – even more than ever – for it is the voice of common sense, of sanity and integrity'. The issues then concerning members of the WI were those with which many members are only too familiar 15 years on. A look at the front cover of the June 1998 issue of *Home & Country* provides an indication of its diverse interests at the end of the 20th century. 'How to look great on a cruise' sits alongside 'Bring crochet into the 90's' (maybe just a little late with only two years left of the decade) and speaks of cosy familiarity with a membership with an older profile. At the same time the front cover also proclaims 'Why the WI is supporting Afghan women' and 'Safeguarding Britain's hedgerows', revealing the concerns of an organisation that was, as ever, ahead of its time.

Climate change, the problems of debt in the developing world, support for British farmers, the loss of local services in the countryside as we saw the mass closure of rural post offices and local shops, road blockades and protests over rising fuel prices, a moratorium on the 'growing and import' of GM foods, the need for detailed food labelling – all these were debated with the prescience that the WI has shown from the outset.

But this decade was also to witness the resurgence of an important part of the WI that was in danger of disappearing under a flood of issue-based campaigning: the opportunity to have fun – the social side of the WI. As Gertrude Wild had written in the first issue of *Home & Country*: 'Life is a fine thing and Institutes are here to help us live it more finely in the future than in the past.' The original aims of the WI were to educate but also to bring communities together in enjoyment. Stand up, the Calendar Girls and the then prime minister. Rylestone and District WI hit the headlines worldwide following their famous calendar, now immortalised in the 2003 film. And at the Triennial General Meeting in 2000 Tony Blair was given a less-than-appreciative response to a long and rambling speech that he will probably never be allowed to forget. Once again the WI was in the news for doing what it had always done – shaking up the establishment.

Gold medal winning WI garden at RHS Tatton to mark the 90th anniversary of WI. The garden was called Back to Our Roots, Growing for Our Future.

The WI and WWF launch a joint campaign against hazardous chemicals

Barbecue-grilled Chicken with Lavender and Thyme

A new series in Home & Country, Feasts from the Vineyard, *is a clue to the growing sophistication of its readers. WI members have always been adventurous when it comes to travel; from early days the magazine carried features on exotic destinations, offering an escape, either in reality or the imagination, for readers stuck at home during challenging times. Carolle Doyle explored the wine region of Roussillon in France, on the border with Catalan Spain, where 'vines cling to steep, parched slopes... and the scent of lavender and thyme hang in the air'. Evocative descriptions of regional specialities sit alongside the recipe below, with recommended wines to try, all from supermarkets. For this dish she suggests a Côtes du Roussillon. Women were increasingly taking over from men as the main wine buyer for the household, putting wine into the trolley as part of their weekly supermarket shop rather than visiting a specialist high street wine merchant.*

Home & Country
1998

**Serves 4 · Preparation 15 minutes, plus marinating
Cook 30 minutes**

8 chicken drumsticks

For the marinade
100ml red wine
4 lavender flowers
finely grated rind of 1 small
    orange
2 fat cloves of garlic, peeled
    and chopped
2 teaspoons fresh thyme,
    chopped
½ teaspoon minced hot chilli
2 teaspoons clear honey
2 tablespoons olive oil
pinch of salt

1   Pour the wine into a stainless steel saucepan and reduce over a steady heat until about two tablespoons remain. Combine the lavender flowers, orange rind, garlic, thyme and chilli in a pestle and mortar or blender. Then add the honey, olive oil, salt and reduced red wine.

2   Slash the drumsticks, cover with the marinade and leave for at least 1 hour, turning once. Preheat a grill or barbecue and allow the embers to settle. Cook the chicken pieces for 15 minutes, turning once. Serve with a salad, crisp French bread and, of course, a glass of red wine.

Ginger Chocolate Brownies

WI cooks like their ginger. It's one ingredient that appears regularly through every decade, and especially and unsurprisingly, in many baking recipes. Whether it's a steamed ginger pudding from the 1920s or a sticky ginger Parkin (see page 29) bulked out with potato during the austerity years of the war, the spice has remained a constant favourite. And its popularity goes even further back. The Romans brought it over here almost two thousand years ago and valued the root for its medicinal properties; the Anglo-Saxons used it in food preparation; and by the late medieval period, it was almost as common as pepper. Stem ginger, as used here, was imported from China sealed in porcelain jars.

Home & Country
2000

Makes 24 · Preparation 15 minutes · Cook 40 minutes

150g dark chocolate, chopped
100g butter
½ tsp vanilla extract
300g caster sugar
4 medium free-range eggs
150g self-raising flour, sifted
50g raisins
75g stem ginger, finely chopped

1 Preheat the oven to 180°C/fan oven 160°C/gas mark 4. Base-line a 27 x 17 x 3cm rectangular tin with baking parchment. Place the chocolate and butter in a basin and either melt in 30 second blasts in the microwave on medium or set the bowl over a pan of gently simmering water. Remember that chocolate melts at body heat so don't overheat or it will seize up. Stir the vanilla extract into the hot chocolate mixture followed by the caster sugar. Stir until melted together.

2 Beat in the eggs one at a time then fold in the flour, raisins and ginger. Pour into the prepared tin and smooth the surface. Bake for 35–40 minutes until the mixture is set but still moist. It should still be gooey in the centre.

3 Cool in the tin on a rack. To serve, cut into 24 squares.

Cooking this recipe today...
The original recipe came iced with glacé icing and a topping of chopped stem ginger but this makes for a very sweet and sickly finish so we have omitted this step. Instead we've upped the chocolate content as we seem to have developed a taste for more intense flavours in the decade or so since the recipe was written. This makes for a gooey brownie that can be eaten straight away, but the ginger flavour will develop if you store them for a day or so. Ideal as a pudding with vanilla ice cream.

Italian Lamb with Roasted Sweet Peppers

Crises in British farming are nothing new to the WI. Hardworking farmers' wives (they were still described in Home & Country *magazine in 2000 as wives rather than as farmers in their own right) have always been active members. A feature in the August 2000 issue celebrated the hard work and initiative shown by four farming members, who, in challenging times for British agriculture, were having to diversify and show 'an enterprising spirit... to keep farming in the family'. Projects included running internet mail-order businesses selling larger-size bras and wooden toys, setting up a farm visitor centre, and producing traditional dry-cured bacon, all of which were helping to support traditional farms through tough times.*

Sadly the countryside was to experience another blow the following year with a devastating outbreak of foot-and-mouth disease. The WI passed a resolution calling on the government to order a full independent investigation into the causes and consequences of the disease. When lamb was back on the menu, this recipe was doubtless a favourite. It's from Debbie Major's Quick Cuisine *series in popular 'recipe card' format.*

Home & Country
2000

Serves 4 · Preparation 15 minutes · Cook 1 hour

750g lean lamb fillet
3 tbsp extra-virgin olive oil
3 cloves garlic, crushed
300ml dry white wine
250ml tomato passata
3 fresh bay leaves
250ml lamb stock
3–4 mixed sweet peppers
salt and freshly ground
   black pepper
egg tagliatelle, to serve

1 Trim off any excess fat from the lamb and cut the flesh into 4cm chunks. Heat the oil in a large pan and brown the lamb on all sides in batches. Return all the lamb to the pan and add the garlic. Stir for a minute.

2 Add the wine and cook over a high heat until it has reduced by a third. Stir in the passata, bay leaves, stock and seasoning and bring to the boil. Half cover the pan and simmer for 1 hour until the sauce is reduced and thick, stirring occasionally.

3 While the lamb is cooking preheat the grill. Put the peppers under the grill, turning now and then until the skins are completely blackened. Place in a plastic bag to cool then rub off the skins. Halve the peppers and remove the seeds. Cut the flesh into wide strips.

4 Add the peppers to the lamb and heat through. Check the seasoning and serve with egg tagliatelle.

Apricot and Almond Crumble

In 1996 spiky-haired chef Gary Rhodes was awarded a second Michelin star for his cooking; this time at The Greenhouse restaurant in Mayfair, not an uncommon phenomenon in a part of London known for its fine dining. But what was unusual was the focus of his menu. British classic dishes such as faggots, braised oxtail and bread and butter pudding may have been familiar to many older WI members, but not to expense-account high-end diners in London's West End. Gary was to spearhead a revolution in catering that is still continuing today – the retro or nostalgic recipe.

Members of the WI had long continued to champion many of these dishes. But interestingly in all the many books spanning the century, there are only a very few recipes for that classic of classics, the simple crumble. Until recently, most women would have learnt to make a crumble from their mothers at an early age, so there was no need for a recipe to be written down. In 2002 Puddings and Desserts *in the* Best-kept Secrets *series included two versions: Apricot and Almond Crumble was given alongside the archetypal blackberry and apple version.*

Best-kept Secrets of the WI: Puddings and Desserts 2002

Serves 6 · Preparation 20 minutes · Cook 25 minutes

675g fresh ripe apricots, halved
   and stoned
25g granulated sugar
175g plain flour
75g caster sugar
50g blanched almonds,
   chopped roughly
50g butter, melted

1 Preheat the oven to 180°C/fan oven 160°C/gas mark 4. Place the apricots, cut side down, in the bottom of a buttered 1-litre baking dish. Sprinkle over the granulated sugar.

2 Combine the flour, caster sugar and almonds in a bowl, pour over the melted butter and stir to form a rough crumble. Spoon evenly over the apricots and bake in the oven for 25 minutes until the crumble topping is golden. Serve warm with custard, cream or vanilla ice cream.

'Some of us might not have specific skills to share, but what we all have in common is that we enjoy getting together and trying new things.'
Darling Roses WI member

Gipsy Creams

According to the introduction to this recipe, no WI biscuit collection would be complete without this acclaimed biscuit. It has even appeared on Channel 4's Countdown quiz – it was presenter the late Richard Whiteley's favourite treat. A manufactured version, produced by McVities even has its very own thread on the Digital Spy forum on the internet, where the passing of the oat and chocolate filled sandwich biscuit is much lamented. Here is the WI's own recipe...

Best-kept Secrets of the WI: Cakes and Biscuits 2002

Makes 16 · Preparation 15 minutes · Cook 20–25 minutes

50g butter
50g lard
50g caster sugar
100g self-raising flour, sifted
1 tbsp cocoa powder, sifted
50g rolled oats
2 tbsp golden syrup dissolved
   in 1 tbsp hot water

For the filling:
25g butter
50g icing sugar, sifted
1 tbsp cocoa powder
few drops vanilla extract

1 Preheat the oven to 180°C/fan oven 160°C/gas mark 4. Cream together the butter, lard and sugar until pale and fluffy then slowly work in the flour, cocoa, oats and golden syrup.

2 Roll the mixture into balls the size of a large cherry. Place on greased baking sheets and flatten with a fork dipped in water to stop it sticking to the dough. Bake for 20–25 minutes until puffy and set.

3 Cool on the trays for 5 minutes then transfer to wire racks to cool completely.

4 For the filling, cream the butter and work in the icing sugar. Beat until light then beat in the chocolate powder and vanilla. Use to sandwich the biscuits together.

'For younger people like myself who are based in cities and work full time and seem to have all the stresses in the world, I would encourage to join for a sense of community.' **Buns & Roses WI member**

Lemon Curd

Preserve-making champion and author Midge Thomas was an occasional tutor at Denman, the spiritual home of WI cooks, and a WI member since the age of 16. She brought her considerable expertise to bear in many WI books on preserving and her name is synonymous with jam making. This particular recipe is apparently one of Midge's favourites. The original recipe came to her from HMSO's Bulletin 21 publication, when she was at college in 1963. It's one of those rare recipes that works really well in a microwave. Midge's original recipe made nearly three kilos of curd so we've cut it down, unless you are making it as a gift or for use in recipes, it doesn't keep longer than a week. As well as being perfect on toast and with scones, lemon curd makes a wonderful filling for cakes and Swiss rolls, can be stirred into whipped cream to sandwich meringues, or folded into yogurt. Midge's preserving recipes continue to have a life of their own, and a new collection, Homemade Jams and Chutneys, *came out in 2012.*

Best-kept Secrets of the WI: Jams, Pickles and Chutneys 2002

**Makes about 1kg (around 3 jars) · Preparation 15 minutes
Cook 8–10 minutes in microwave or 40 minutes on the hob**

100g butter
350g sugar, granulated
  or caster
grated rind of 2–3 lemons
150ml lemon juice (from
  2–3 lemons)
150ml beaten eggs (about
  2–3 free-range eggs or
  2–3 egg yolks plus 1 egg)

1 Place the butter, sugar, lemon rind and juice in a medium bowl and microwave on full power for a minute in 30-second bursts until the butter has melted and the sugar dissolved.

2 Add the beaten eggs and keep microwaving in 20–30 second bursts, stirring after each and reducing the time to 15 seconds as the mixture thickens, until the curd is thick enough to coat the back of a wooden spoon. (To make on the hob, put all the ingredients in a bowl set over a pan of hot water. Once the butter has melted and the sugar dissolved, stir the mixture until thick enough to coat back of wooden spoon – about 15 minutes.)

3 Strain the curd through a sieve into a wide-necked jug to remove the lemon rind and any egg bits. Pour into cool sterilised jars and cover with wax discs and cellophane. Leave to cool then store for up to 10 days in the fridge.

For passion-fruit curd add the seeds and pulp of two passion fruit just before potting. For elderflower curd carefully strip the tiny flowers from the stems of 2 handfuls of elderflowers and add to the curd when cooking.

Brazil Nut and Apricot Bread

An iconic series of paperback cookery books – Best-kept Secrets of the WI – saw a fresh look to the WI's publications for the new millennium. Titles highlighted the cooking knowledge and skills for which the WI is renowned. The colourful books covered the full range from Breads and Jams, Pickles and Chutneys to Soups, from Chocolate to Cakes and Biscuits. And they introduced a whole raft of new cooks to the organisation's way with classic and modern recipes that not only worked every time but, with their accessible ingredients and clear methods, reassured the more inexperienced cook while delighting the traditionalists.

Following guidelines on healthy eating at the time, many recipes specify margarine over butter, even for classics such as scones where butter makes such a difference to flavour. In the years since these books were published, recent health advice is starting to take us back to cooking with less processed, old-fashioned fats such as butter, lard and even dripping, as used by our grandmothers' generation of bakers. This light fruit bread is made with butter and goes well with a cheese board.

Best-kept Secrets of the WI: Bread & Bakes 2003

Makes one 900g loaf · Preparation 20 minutes, plus rising Cook 25–35 minutes

450g strong white bread flour, plus extra for dusting
1 tsp salt
25g butter
25g caster sugar
1 tsp easy-blend dried yeast
100g soft apricots, roughly chopped
75g Brazil nuts, roughly chopped
200ml hand-hot water
150ml hand-hot milk

1 Sift the flour and salt into a large mixing bowl and quickly rub in the butter with your fingertips. Add the sugar and yeast. Stir in the apricots and nuts.

2 Mix the water and milk and add to the dry ingredients. Stir together to form a soft dough.

3 Turn the dough onto a lightly floured work surface and knead until smooth and elastic. Place in a clean oiled bowl and cover with cling film. Leave in a warm place until doubled in size.

4 Turn the dough onto a floured surface and knock out the air. Knead quickly until smooth then shape and fit into a 900g greased loaf tin. Cover with oiled cling film and leave to rise for 30 minutes until doubled in size.

5 Preheat the oven to 200°C/fan oven 180°C/gas mark 6. Bake for 25–35 minutes until golden and hollow sounding when tapped on the base. Transfer to a wire rack to cool.

'Members from all walks of life have such amazing stories to tell and talents to share, a truly inspiring group of women.' **Stroud Green WI member**

Thai Red Prawn Curry with Basil

The start of the new millennium saw a huge explosion of interest in cooking from South Asia, as countries such as Thailand opened their boarders to tourists. TV chefs travelled far and wide for inspiration. The arrival of fusion food saw the introduction of new ingredients into everyday shopping baskets. Home & Country *magazine moved with the times and had already recruited cookery writers such as Debbie Major, long-time collaborator with television chef Rick Stein, to contribute to the magazine, alongside the WI's own Rosemary Wadey in place since 1969.*

Debbie's recipe for Thai prawn curry appeared as part of a feature on using fresh basil, and reflects the huge rise in popularity of Thai cooking. Back then cooks might be lucky to find one or two curry pastes even in a specialist Thai supermarket, but now we are in danger of being spoiled for choice. Debbie even suggests going to the trouble of searching out Thai holy basil, quite a challenge at the time for rural WI cooks.

*Home & Country
2003*

Serves 4 · Preparation 10 minutes · Cook 15 minutes

2 tbsp sunflower oil
5cm piece fresh ginger, peeled and shredded
3 cloves garlic, thinly sliced
1 medium onion, finely chopped
2–3 tbsp Thai red curry paste
400g can coconut milk
2 tsp light brown sugar
juice of 1 lime
2 tbsp light soy sauce
100ml fish or chicken stock
300g peeled raw tiger prawns
100g mange tout, cut in half on the diagonal
200g can bamboo shoots, drained and rinsed
leaves from a small bunch of fresh basil

1　Heat the oil in a large pan, add the ginger and garlic and cook for a minute, then add the onion and cook over a medium heat for 3–4 minutes until soft and golden.

2　Add the curry paste and cook for 2 minutes, then stir in the coconut milk, sugar, lime juice, soy sauce and stock and simmer for 2 minutes. Add the prawns and simmer for another couple of minutes. Stir in the mange tout and bamboo shoots and continue cooking until the prawns are cooked through and the mange tout are just tender.

3　Stir in the torn basil leaves and serve with plenty of steamed Thai rice.

Stilton Soup with Broccoli

The WI has flown the flag for local cooking throughout its existence, and been instrumental in keeping alive many culinary traditions that, in this age of globalisation and homogenised high streets, might have been lost to us. This recipe from the East Midlands (alongside ones for Melton Mowbray Pie and Sage Derby Soufflés), appeared in the November 2003 issue of Home & Country magazine as part of a series by Rosemary Wadey on Cooking Around Britain. It demonstrates the commitment to local food producers and ingredients that has always been at the forefront of the WI. As Rosemary reminds us in her introduction, 'Stilton, like champagne, has protected status – it can only be made in the counties of Leicestershire, Nottinghamshire and Derbyshire'.

Instead of thickening the soup with flour, as in the original soup, we have upped the cheese and broccoli content to make a richer, more satisfying soup that has the wonderfully distinctive cheese at its heart.

Home & Country
2003

Serves 4 · Preparation 15 minutes · Cook 20 minutes

30g butter
1 large onion, finely chopped
2 sticks celery, chopped
1 clove garlic, crushed
300g broccoli, including stalks, roughly chopped
600ml chicken or vegetable stock
300ml semi-skimmed milk
100g Stilton, crumbled
juice of half a lemon
salt and freshly ground black pepper
yogurt or crème fraîche, to serve

1   Melt the butter in a large pan and add the onion, celery and garlic. Cook for 5 minutes over a gentle heat until the vegetables have softened but are not coloured.

2   Add the broccoli and stir together for a minute then add the stock, milk and seasoning and bring to the boil. Simmer gently for 10–12 minutes until the broccoli is tender, then add the Stilton. Whizz up in a blender, or use a hand-held stick blender in the pan, to create a smooth soup. Check seasoning and add lemon juice to taste, then serve in warmed bowls with a spoonful of yogurt or crème fraîche.

Mushroom Strudel

After the food scares of this (and the previous) decade, increasing numbers of people began reducing their meat intake, with twice as many women becoming vegetarian compared to men. Growing numbers of cooks were catering for mixed groups of both vegetarians and meat eaters at Christmas. This was reflected in cookery publications such as the WI Complete Christmas book of 2004, with a chapter dedicated specifically to vegetarian dishes, moving on from the ubiquitous nut roast to more sophisticated offerings such as this Mushroom Strudel, using the increasingly wide range of vegetarian-friendly products. (By 2009 the UK had the third highest rate of vegetarians in the European Union.)

WI Complete
Christmas
2004

Makes 2 strudels · Serves 6 · Preparation 30 minutes Cook 35 minutes

175g butter
1 small onion, finely chopped
1 garlic clove, crushed
125g button mushrooms, sliced
150g chestnut mushrooms, sliced
225g flat mushrooms, sliced
1 tablespoon sherry
1 tsp fresh thyme leaves
25g fresh white breadcrumbs
25g pine nuts, toasted
8 small sheets filo pastry
3 tablespoons cranberry sauce
1 tablespoon sesame seeds
salt and freshly ground black pepper
fresh thyme sprigs, to garnish

1   Melt half the butter in a large saucepan and fry the onion and garlic gently until soft. Add all the mushrooms and toss well together. Fry for a few minutes until cooked. Off the heat, stir in the sherry, thyme, breadcrumbs, pine nuts and seasoning. Leave to cool.

2   Preheat the oven to 200°C/fan oven 180°C/gas mark 6. Melt the remaining butter and lay a tea towel on the work surface. Arrange a sheet of filo on top with the longest side closest to you. Brush with butter and add three more layers of filo, buttering as you go.

3   Spread half the cranberry sauce over the pastry. Spoon half the mushroom mixture along the side furthest away from you leaving a gap at either end. Fold in the ends over the filling, and using the towel to help you, roll the strudel towards you until you have a neat parcel.

4   Lift the strudel onto a large baking sheet, brush with butter and sprinkle with half the sesame seeds. Repeat the process to make a second strudel. Bake for 30–35 minutes until crisp and golden brown, covering loosely with foil if it browns too quickly.

WI members marching to raise awareness of climate
change in the People's Climate March,
2014

2006–2015

The new age of austerity

A fter a couple of decades' hiatus with a slowly declining
membership that still saw the movement continue to quietly
fulfill its remit as educator, supporter and social hub for women
across Britain (the Big Society is nothing new to the members of the
WI), this is the decade that has witnessed a resurgence for the
WI – both from within and as seen by the wider public.

As had happened in the post-war years, a new membership – there are currently more than 212,000 members and the number is growing every week – has started to push at the boundaries of the organisation. WIs in town and cities meet in pubs and coffee shops, and new workplace and university institutes run craft and cookery sessions that provide practical skills to women of all ages and backgrounds. Many of the more traditional WIs are eagerly embracing the digital age to refresh their approach to recruiting new members, and opening up new opportunities for celebrating friendship and promoting local causes and endeavours.

The financial crisis of 2008 caused many of us to focus inwards on our home life and to re-evaluate our priorities. The fallout from this is only really being recognised now. The new austerity, concerns about climate change, overpopulation and declining resources, and the anniversary of the start of the First World War, have all served to encourage us to look back at our heritage, and reinterpret its messages for the new millennium. The WI is being recognised as a vital repository of valuable skills and knowledge.

In these stressful times we take comfort from traditional pastimes and time spent in our communities and with our friends. Interest in craft skills is booming, baking, sewing and gardening shows have overtaken television schedules (often with WI members in key roles as experts), and we are making the most of new methods of communication through everything from social media to podcasts and pop-up events to share these simple pleasures.

Volunteering is finally being recognised as not only being good for society but for creating bonds and enhancing life as we move towards an ageing population. And the WI is in a good place to face the challenges of the new century and provide a bedrock of wisdom and flexibility that has stood the WI in good stead over the past century.

'Joining the WI and helping the Scouts could save your life, academics have found.'
2013 *The Daily Telegraph*

Top line left to right
WI members celebrating the summer of sport, 2012

Members of Buns and Roses WI in Leeds, 2011

Middle line
Anna Tebble from Seven Hills WI cooking at the WI Cookery School, 2013

Bottom line left to right
WI member taking part in the Little Black Dress ethical fashion show, 2011

Guinness World Record knitting attempt at the NFWI AGM in the Royal Albert Hall, 2012

Banana Banoffee Muffins

Muffins have transformed in the lifetime of the WI. Close relations to the crumpet (which first appeared in printed recipe form in Hannah Glasse's The Art of Cookery *in 1747), we're now obliged to refer to our traditional yeast-leavened bread disks cooked on a griddle as English muffins. This is to distinguish them from the even more popular cake-style American muffin, cooked in its own paper case, and ubiquitous in the US.*

With the arrival on these shores of the American-style coffee shop (the first Starbucks opened in London in 1998), we have embraced the sweet cakey muffin and now eat it at all times of the day. Lately it has come up against strong competition from the cupcake, with its sweet buttercream topping, but the American muffin continues to hold its own. It can be sweet, savoury, warm or cold, served with butter or jam. This version incorporates another 21st-century phenomenon, banoffee flavour. Serve cold or warm as a pudding with ice cream.

WI: Cakes
2009

Makes 10 · Preparation 15 minutes · Cook 25 minutes

225g plain flour
1½ tsp baking powder
½ tsp bicarbonate of soda
150g golden caster sugar
2 medium ripe bananas, mashed
2 medium free-range eggs, beaten
4 tbsp soured cream
½ tsp vanilla extract
80g butter, melted and cooled
10 tsp dulce de leche sauce or caramel toffee

1 Preheat the oven to 190°C/fan oven 170°C/gas mark 5. Line a muffin tin with ten paper cases. Sift the flour, baking powder and bicarbonate of soda into a mixing bowl. Stir in the caster sugar.

2 Make a well in the centre of the dry ingredients and add the bananas, eggs, soured cream, vanilla extract and melted butter. Fold together gently until just combined. Spoon into the muffin cases and place a spoonful of the toffee sauce on the centre of each muffin.

3 Bake for 20–25 minutes until the mixture is just risen, golden and firm to touch. The toffee sauce will melt down through the muffin as it cooks. Transfer to wire racks to cool. Serve warm or cold.

'The common thread running through all WI campaigns has been a strong appreciation of the need for social and environmental justice, combined with a willingness to take action to achieve it.'
Ruth Bond, NFWI Chair 2009–2013

The Lemony Tart

When Madge Watt set up the WI a hundred years ago, one of her most important reasons was to give local women a forum for making friends. Today social media makes that process a lot easier for many of us, and new-style WIs are embracing technology to reach potential members in both rural and urban settings. In 2010 new mum Rebecca Cobb-Kilner found herself at home in Huddersfield with a baby, and no friends within a 20-mile radius. The WI was recommended as a possible solution to her problem, so she decided to take action. And from small beginnings the Tea and Tarts WI grew to its current membership of more than 75 women.

Rebecca says: 'Tea & Tarts is one of the new WIs that is introducing women of all ages to traditional and not so traditional skills. One month you'll find us perfecting our needlework and the next we're bustin' some moves to lowdown dirty hippity hop.' The colourful website with its graphic mascot, The Eponymous Lemony Tart, is in keeping with a long history of design capabilities that has seen WI members illustrate, design and write their own publications, and greets potential new members with the promise that 'whether you are confident in new surroundings or an honest to goodness wallflower, The Tarts will offer you a welcome.'

Tea and Tarts WI
2010

Makes 6 · Preparation 30 minutes, plus chilling
Cook 15–18 minutes

For the pastry:
200g unsalted butter
1 large free-range egg yolk
50g icing sugar
1 tbsp double cream
250g plain flour, plus extra
   for dusting

For the filling:
Lemon Curd (see page 186)
175ml double cream

1   Use a food processor to make the pastry. Blend the butter, egg yolk, icing sugar and cream together for 30 seconds. Add the flour and blend until the dough becomes a ball. Divide it into six pieces, pat them flat, wrap and pop in the fridge for 1 hour.

2   Flour the work surface and roll out each piece to a 15cm circle. Prick all over with a fork. Carefully lift the dough and pop into a small individual tart tin (10cm). Gently press the dough into the tin without stretching it. Do the same with all the dough. Freeze for at least 30 minutes before baking.

3   Preheat the oven to 190°C/fan oven 170°C/gas mark 5. Bake for 15–18 minutes. The pastry should be golden. Carefully remove the pastry cases from the tins and leave to cool.

4   Whisk the cream until stiff and fold gently into the lemon curd. Spoon into the pastry cases. Serve to good friends, or perfect strangers, with Lady Grey Tea in dainty china cups.

Steamed Fish with Ginger and White Wine

In 1917 Sussex was one of the earliest WI federations to be established; two years later it divided into West and East. Forest Row was one of the earliest of East Sussex's 102 WIs and can trace its history back to the 1920s. During the Great Depression of the 1930s it ran an active WI market, but 60 years later membership was decreasing, and it closed. In late 2010 several local women saw the need for a way to strengthen links between women in the village and re-establishing the Forest Row WI seemed a perfect solution. The inaugural meeting – the 'new face of the WI' – was promoted on Facebook, promising new ideas and fun for 'vibrant, proactive' women. Thirty women came to that first meeting.

In early 2011 the first official meeting was a good example of the way new members are making the WI their own. The new village fishmongers gave a demonstration on preparing and cooking fish to an audience of more than 70 enthusiastic women. This recipe comes from president Catherine Smith, inspired by that inaugural meeting.

Forest Row WI 2011

Serves 4 · Preparation 20 minutes · Cook 15 minutes

500g firm white fish, such as haddock or brill (or try sustainable gurnard fillet)
2 medium carrots, cut into matchsticks
2 sticks celery, cut into matchsticks
1 small onion
1 red pepper
1.5cm piece fresh root ginger, peeled and cut into matchsticks
2 tbsp fresh lemon juice
3 tbsp dry white wine
4 tbsp double cream or crème fraîche
salt and freshly ground black pepper

1 Cut the fish into generous chunks. Take four pieces of buttered foil, and divide the vegetables between them. Place the fish on top. Sprinkle over the lemon juice and white wine and season with salt and pepper.

2 Gather together the corners of the foil and seal into four parcels. Place flat in a steamer and cook over simmering water for 10–12 minutes.

3 Open the parcels and pour off the cooking liquid into a small pan. Close up the foil to keep the fish warm. Add the cream to the liquid and bring to the boil. Season to taste to make a sauce. Serve the fish with the sauce, new potatoes and green beans.

Scones with Variations

Scone recipes have appeared in WI publications from the outset. A Ministry of Food information piece on making the most of precious rations from 1944 recommends rendering down odd bits of fat in order to make 'nice things your family will love' and gives a scone recipe that uses a small amount of carefully harvested margarine with 'household milk', and that could even be padded out with mashed potato to spread treasured ingredients even further.

We still love scones, and with the renewed interest in baking, can try all kinds of styles and recipes, from the traditional cream tea to something more adventurous. Scones are right on trend: ready-made versions are widely available, and a search on the internet for the perfect scone produces thousands of results.

The secret of a good scone is that it's fresh, soft and fluffy, and, for WI members, freshly baked is really the only proper way to enjoy a scone at its very best, warm from the oven. Topped with cream then jam or the other way round, they continue to take centre stage at any special tea party.

*The WI
Vintage Teatime
2012*

Makes 8–10 · Preparation 10 minutes · Cook 15 minutes

225g plain flour
¼ tsp salt
1 tsp cream of tartar
½ tsp bicarbonate of soda
1 tbsp caster sugar (optional)
60g butter, diced
150ml milk or buttermilk
milk, to glaze

1   Preheat the oven to 230°C/fan oven 210°C/gas mark 8. Sift the flour, salt, cream of tartar and bicarbonate of soda into a large mixing bowl. Add the sugar (if using). Rub in the butter until the mixture resembles fine breadcrumbs.

2   Add enough milk or buttermilk to mix to a soft dough with a palette knife. Turn onto a lightly floured work surface. Pat out the dough to 2.5cm thick. Cut out rounds using a well-floured 4cm cutter. Reroll the trimmings and cut more scones.

3   Place on a lightly floured baking sheet. Brush the tops with milk and bake for 12–15 minutes until well risen and golden brown. Transfer to a wire rack to cool.

For fruit scones, add 50g dried fruit such as raisins, sultanas, mixed peel, dried cranberries to the dry ingredients.

For cheese scones, add a large pinch of mustard powder and 50g grated strong Cheddar to the dry ingredients.

Pasta with Meat Sauce and Pomegranate

Things have moved on for the WI in this new century, as the organisation continues to adapt and raise its profile as the largest voluntary membership organisation for women in the UK. In 2006 Home & Country *magazine was relaunched as* WI Life *and remains the organisation's main method of communication. Delivered to all WI members eight times a year, the magazine showcases the full range of opportunities and activities for members, and celebrates their diversity and interests.*

Three years later, the Denman WI Cookery School opened, welcoming members and non-members alike (men and women) for courses on everything from traditional bakery and perfect pastry to sushi workshops and making your own chorizo. Denman tutor Lindy Wildsmith is a regular contributor to the food pages of WI Life, *and in February 2013 the magazine featured recipes from her Trattoria Classics course. Lindy lived near Rome for many years and her love of Italian food is reflected in the range of courses she teaches.*

WI Life
2013

Serves 4–6 · Preparation 15 minutes · Cook 2 hours

handful of wild mushrooms
750ml full-fat milk
olive oil
50g pancetta, finely chopped
1 bunch parsley, finely chopped
1 stick celery, finely chopped
1 small carrot, finely chopped
1 small onion, finely chopped
500g minced steak, shoulder
  of wild boar or venison
300ml red wine
2 tbsp tomato purée
1 fresh bay leaf
freshly grated nutmeg
beef stock as needed
  (see step 3)
seeds from 1 pomegranate
freshly grated Parmesan
salt and freshly ground black
  pepper

1 Soak the wild mushrooms in enough milk to cover generously and leave for 1 hour. Squeeze dry and chop.

2 Heat enough olive oil to cover the base of a large pan, add the pancetta, parsley and chopped vegetables and fry until translucent. Add the minced meat and fry over a high heat until well browned. Add the soaked mushrooms and wine and simmer to evaporate.

3 Add enough milk to cover the meat. Add the tomato purée, bay leaf, nutmeg and seasoning. Stir well and simmer, covered, for at least 2 hours, stirring in stock to keep the sauce moist as needed, until rich and thick. Leave to stand for 20 minutes or overnight.

4 To serve heat through and stir into *al dente* egg tagliatelle with plenty of freshly grated Parmesan. Transfer to a warm serving dish and scatter with the pomegranate seeds. Serve with extra wedges of pomegranate on the side of the dish if desired.

'We all want every WI to be everything the members want it to be and to do this we have to be sure the WI is here to inspire its members so that we can all be inspiring women working together. At the end of the day, the WI is what you make of it.'
Janice Langley, NFWI Chair in 2015

Honeyed Lamb Shoulder

Over the past 50 years, our consumption of cheaper meat cuts and offal has dwindled to practically nothing. A weariness with the restrictions of rationing after the war years, scares such as foot-and-mouth and BSE, and the increasing pressure on time for working women had seen these items fall from favour with many home cooks. But the current economic crisis has sent us back to old recipe books in the search for comfort food at sensible prices and traditional specialists such as old-fashioned master butchers.

Our WI grandmothers would have been horrified at the waste in modern households: they not only made full use of every thing in their larders and fridges but sought out ingredients and cuts of meat that often needed little preparation apart from a long slow cooking time. The past few years have seen a resurgence in demand for many of these forgotten cuts, and this recipe for a shoulder of lamb is a good example. Ask your butcher or supermarket meat counter to bone out the shoulder and roll and tie it.

Woman's World Magazine 2013

Serves 6 · Preparation 10 minutes · Cook 2½ hours

1 tbsp oil

1.35kg boneless lamb
  shoulder joint

3 cloves garlic

2 large sprigs mint,
  roughly torn

2 large sprigs thyme,
  roughly torn

grated rind and juice of 1 lemon

2 tbsp honey

150ml apple juice or cider

500g new potatoes, halved

6 baby leeks or 2 medium leeks,
  cut into chunks

salt and freshly ground black
  pepper

1 Preheat the oven to 180°C/fan oven 160°C/gas mark 4. Heat the oil in a flameproof casserole or deep roasting tin large enough to fit the joint with room around it. Add the joint and brown it well on all sides. Add the garlic, mint, thyme, lemon rind, juice and seasoning to the pan, followed by the honey and apple juice or cider.

2 Cover the pan with its lid or a double layer of foil, sealing the edges securely. Cook for 1 hour. Remove the lid and add the potatoes and leeks to the pan, stirring them into the juices. Return to the oven for a further hour until the meat is tender and well browned, and the vegetables are cooked through.

3 Rest the joint for at least 15 minutes then slice thickly and serve with the vegetables and pan juices, strained and spooned over the meat.

Plum and Mulled Wine Jam

In December 2010, Denman launched the WI Real Jam Festival, which ran for four years before pausing for the centenary celebrations throughout 2015. The festival includes preserving demonstrations in the WI Cookery School, craft displays and a Christmas market, alongside competition classes to suit all abilities, from children through to chefs and bloggers and even a special class just for men. Classes include best strawberry jam, best boozy jelly or jam and Christmas chutney – the perfect opportunity for the nation's preserving fans to talk to other 'jammies' and measure themselves against the best. Jars are sent in from around the country ready for the intense three-day judging process: in 2013 there were 330 jars of jams, jellies and chutneys.

This recipe from Midge Thomas's book is adapted from the set recipe for one of the 2013 classes. Use a reasonable quality red wine, such as a Merlot, for a good flavour.

Women's Institute
Homemade Jams and Chutney
2013

Makes 6 x 450g jars · Preparation 20 minutes
Cook 50 minutes

1.8kg red plums, halved and
 stoned
375ml red wine
mulled wine spices (a cinnamon
 stick, whole nutmeg and
 several cloves)
1 large piece of orange rind
 without pith
1.8kg granulated sugar

1 Put the plums and wine in a large preserving pan. Place the spices and rind in a spice ball or tie in a muslin bag, and add to the pan. Bring to the boil and simmer gently for 15–20 minutes or until the plum skins are soft.

2 Remove the spice ball or bag and add the sugar, stirring over a gentle heat until completely dissolved. Do not allow to boil until the sugar has completely dissolved.

3 Bring to the boil and boil rapidly for about 10 minutes or until setting point is reached. Remove any scum with a slotted spoon. Pour into cooled, sterilised jars. Seal and label. Store in a cool, dark place.

'I can honestly say that by joining the WI I feel that I have made friends and become part of the community.' **Wimbledon WI member**

Couscous with Beans, Feta and Olives

This recipe is adapted from one that appears on the current WI website (which came originally from Healthy Heart – one of the latest Best-kept Secrets of the WI series). It reveals our ongoing concerns with what makes a healthy diet, at a time when we are constantly bombarded with advice, reports and research – often conflicting. Salt and fat are key enemies, as concerns about rising obesity levels and high blood pressure grow. Food labelling and hidden salt found in everyday foods hit the headlines with increasing regularity, creating a confusing environment for the consumer trying to do her best to feed her family and herself. As ever, the WI is a sensible informed presence. The introduction to this recipe states, 'it does include cheese but feta is not one of the highest in fat content. However it can be fairly salty, as are the olives; so rinse the olives well and don't add additional salt to the recipe to keep the content down.'

WI website 2014

Serves 4–6 · Preparation 15 minutes · Cook 10 minutes

250g couscous
400g can chickpeas, rinsed and drained
400g can borlotti beans, rinsed and drained
200g cherry tomatoes, halved
100g black olives, stoned, rinsed and drained
200g feta cheese, cubed
2 tbsp chopped fresh mint
2 tbsp chopped flat-leaved parsley
3 tbsp extra-virgin olive oil
3 tbsp lemon juice
freshly ground black pepper

1   Place the couscous in a large bowl and pour over 350ml boiling water. Stir, then leave to stand for 10 minutes to allow the grains to swell and absorb the water. Fork through to loosen up the couscous.

2   Gently stir in all the other ingredients and mix well to combine. Season to taste with black pepper and transfer to a large serving dish.

3   The dish can be chilled slightly before serving but remove from the fridge ahead of serving to allow the flavours to develop. It will keep for 2 days in the fridge in an airtight container.

For non-vegetarian diners, leftover cooked meat or fish could also be added, as well as small amounts of veg you have in the fridge. Try adding a tablespoon or two of harissa paste for added zing.

Venison Steaks with Quick Béarnaise Sauce

Such has been the popularity of the WI as a social glue that many areas of the country have several institutes within a small area. The small East Sussex village of Hartfield had two in the village, with an afternoon group and one that met in the evening for working women. These amalgamated into one back in 1976 (of which the author is a member). The village sits on the edge of the Ashdown Forest, and takes its name from the deer that still graze up on the forest.

In the past decade game has returned to family menus, as its lean free-range meat fits into modern concerns about healthy eating and local food sourcing. Whilst our grandmothers would be more likely to casserole venison with spices and red wine, put the meat in a pie, or maybe roast a saddle, we do things differently today. Modern venison is very lean, hung for just long enough to tenderise and improve flavour. To be enjoyed at their best, the prime cuts need fast and simple cooking; treat them the same way as you would the best beef. This version of a classic steak is a good way to introduce newcomers to the meat.

Hartfield &
Medway WI
2014

Serves 4 · Preparation 10 minutes · Cook 15–20 minutes

1 tsp black peppercorns,
   coarsely ground
1 tbsp olive oil
4 venison fillet steaks, about
   150g each

For the béarnaise sauce:
2 tbsp white wine vinegar
6 black peppercorns
1 shallot, finely chopped
2 large free-range egg yolks
100g unsalted butter
grated rind and juice of
   ½ lemon

1 Press the crushed pepper onto both sides of the steaks. Heat the oil in a ridged griddle pan or non-stick frying pan and cook the steaks on both sides, turning once, for 4–6 minutes for rare, 8–10 minutes for medium and 10–12 minutes for well done. (Timings will also vary depending on the thickness of the steaks.) Remove from the pan and leave to stand in a warm place for 5–10 minutes for the juices to settle.

2 Prepare the béarnaise sauce. Place the vinegar in a small pan with the peppercorns, shallot and 2 tablespoons water. Bring to the boil and simmer until the vinegar is reduced to 1 tablespoon.

3 Strain the reduced vinegar onto the egg yolk and blend briefly to mix. Heat the butter in a small pan until really bubbling but not browned. With the blender running, pour the hot butter on the egg yolks in a steady stream. The sauce should be thick and creamy. Stir in the lemon rind and the juice, season to taste and serve immediately with the steaks.

Centenary Celebration Cake

To celebrate one hundred years of the WI, what could be more appropriate than a baking competition? And this particular challenge was for members to come up with a homemade celebration fruit cake recipe to be served up to the most exacting judges – all those present at the 100th Annual General Meeting of the WI, taking place in the Royal Albert Hall itself in June 2015! Not only will every member present in the hall on the day be able to taste and comment, the whole event is being beamed nationwide to institutes to join in the festivities live via cinema screens and online.

Back in 2014 members were asked to send in their recipes to be judged by the NFWI Education Committee. After much careful baking and tasting a winner was selected – and here it is for you to try at home. The recipe appears exactly as it was written by winning baker Julie Clark of North Yorks West Federation. Well done, Julie!

N Yorks West Federation 2014

Makes a 20cm-square cake · Preparation 30 minutes Cook 4–4½ hours

225g (8oz) butter, slightly softened
225g (8oz) soft dark brown sugar
4 large free-range eggs
175g (6oz) plain flour
55g (2oz) self-raising flour
80g (3oz) ground almonds
80g (3oz) glace cherries, cut into quarters
400g (14oz) currants, small pinhead
170g (6oz) sultanas
55g (2oz) mixed cut peel
½ tbsp marmalade
a wineglass of rum

1 Line a 20cm square tin with a double layer of non-stick baking parchment.

2 Make a collar of folded newspaper for the outside of the tin, plus a thick piece of newspaper for the cake to sit on.

3 Cream the butter and sugar until light and fluffy.

4 Beat in the eggs, then stir in the flours and ground almonds.

5 Fold in the fruits, followed by the marmalade and rum. Make sure all ingredients are well mixed.

6 Transfer to the cake tin and smooth the top.

7 Bake the cake at 160°C/fan oven 140°C/gas mark 3.

8 Turn down the heat after ½–¾ hour to 150°C/fan oven 130°C/gas mark 2 and bake until cooked – anywhere between 2–3½ hours.

9 Use your common sense and turn down the oven as necessary if the cake is getting too brown.

—◦◦◦◦—

*'The Women's Institute has a special kind of power...
You can make change happen. You campaign for the
things you believe in. Whether it is the environment,
food labelling or women's rights, the root of your
campaigning is always the same, driving out
ignorance and changing people's minds through
education, information and better understanding.'*
Annie Mauger, Chief Executive, CILIP, 2011 AGM

'The WI is such a positive energy hub which has enabled me to take advantage of creative opportunities as well as widening my horizons through contact with other participants, members and with current issues highlighted through the targeted campaigns.' **Wanstead WI member**

Index

(page numbers in italic type refer to photographs)

WI members taking part in a gardening class,
1961

Mary Gwynn's acknowledgements

The researching and writing of this book has been an honour for me to undertake. The opportunity to get under the skin of the extraordinary organisation that is the WI has taken up over a year of my life, and encompassed all the ups and downs that go hand-in-hand with such a project, especially one that changed publishers midway through.

Huge thanks are due to all those who have supported and helped me throughout. The whole publishing team at Ebury, but most especially Nicki Crossley who has held the whole thing together under pressure, and ensured that we have finished up with a book worthy of all the women (past and present) of the WI, but also the calm and wonderful Sharon Amos, and the design and photography teams who have worked wonders with a complex format.

And to my recipe testers, Isobel Curtis and Penny Young, who have worked to ensure the old and new work well for modern cooks; to Heather Holden Brown, Elly James and Jack Munnelly who have been unfailingly supportive and encouraging, and to Loz Jerram, who got the initial concept on the path to publication.

At the NFWI my gratitude and thanks go to the Board of Trustees for their support for the book but most especially to Janice Langley and Diana Birch for their own championing of it from start to finish, and to the NFWI staff team at headquarters, who have made me welcome, given me access to the fascinating and extensive archive and fed me cups of tea and very welcome sandwiches as I pored over old magazines, books and leaflets. And to the members who have sent me recipes in response to my appeals on Facebook.

Finally thanks to my partner and family who have lived day in and day out with the WI and my enthusiasm and (occasional!) frustration with all its marvelous history over the past century.

The WI's acknowledgements

Looking back over the past 100 years of WI cookery would not have been possible without the dedication of our author and WI member, Mary Gwynn. Mary has spent long hours searching through our archives, examining the vast number of historical WI recipe texts, educational food documents and leaflets offering advice on everything from what to do with your leftovers, to how to cook a balanced meal for your family when faced with rationing restrictions. She has brought together some of the best recipes that the WI has to offer which form the backbone of the book, and demonstrate how both the organisation and the country have changed and developed over the past century in their approach to the food we buy, cook and eat.

Special thanks must go to the NFWI's agent, Juliet Pickering at Blake Friedmann, who stepped into the breach just when she was needed, and really made sure that we ended up with such a fabulous book at the end of it all. Thank you, Juliet.

For providing such beautiful images, thanks go to photographer Jan Baldwin and art director Mary Norden. The food styling by Emma Marsden really brings these recipes to life and they all look delicious. Their vision and determination have resulted in images that really do look good enough to eat!

Sincere thanks to the team at Ebury; Sharon Amos and Laura Nickoll for editing the text and making sure that we have a book to be rightly proud to celebrate our centenary, and to Nicola Crossley for making sure everything that needed to be done was done on time. Thanks also go to the design team at Two Associates for ensuring that the book looks just as we all hoped; a great testament to the first 100 years of WI cookery.

From within the NFWI team, special thanks must go to Diana Birch and Janice Langley and to the entire Board of Trustees who have supported the project from the beginning to make sure that the WI had a book to celebrate with in 2015. Thanks to the NFWI staff team of Jana Osborne, Mark Linacre and Hilary Ransom who drove the project forward in the midst of centenary project planning, and to Charlotte Fiander for the editorial and image advice and ensuring that the WI voice rang true throughout.

Last but not least, we must say a huge thank you to WI members both past and present who have helped make this book what it is, by creating recipes across the century that reflect their times and concerns so wonderfully. This book belongs to all of you, and we hope you enjoy creating dishes from the past 100 years as much as we have enjoyed compiling them. The strength of the WI lies in its members, and this book is for each and every one.

Top left:
Wartime fruit preservation centre in 1940

Top right:
Keep fit demonstration at the 1984 Annual General Meeting outside the Royal Albert Hall

Middle right:
WI delegates at the AGM at the Royal Albert Hall

Bottom left:
Tea time at Denman

Bottom right:
Lunch on the steps outside the Royal Albert Hall at the AGM in 1971

3 5 7 9 10 8 6 4 2

Ebury Press, an imprint of Ebury Publishing,
20 Vauxhall Bridge Road,
London SW1V 2SA

Ebury Press is part of the Penguin Random House group of companies whose addresses
can be found at global.penguinrandomhouse.com

www.eburypublishing.co.uk

A CIP catalogue record for this book is available from the British Library

ISBN 978 1 785 03047 5

Printed and bound by Firmengruppe APPL, aprinta druck, Wemding, Germany
Repro by AltaImage

Design by Two Associates
Food Photography by Jan Baldwin
Art Direction by Mary Norden
Food Styling by Emma Marsden
Editing by Sharon Amos and Laura Nickoll
Project Management by Nicki Crossley

Photography credits
All food photography by Jan Baldwin. All archive images care of the National Federation of Women's Institutes,
with the exception to those mentioned below:
Page 176 © Henry Iddon. Page 194 © Mat Banks. Page 197 Top line left to right, WI members celebrating the
summer of sport 2012 © Paul Webb. Members of Buns and Roses WI in Leeds 2011 © Peter Schiazza. Middle
line, Anna Tebble from Seven Hills WI cooking at the WI Cookery School 2013 © Lindsay Garfitt, Bottom line,
WI member taking part in the Little Black Dress ethical fashion show 2011 © Iain Weir. Guinness World record
knitting attempt at the NFWI AGM in the Royal Albert Hall 2012, © Andy Lane.

Penguin Random House is committed to a sustainable future for our business, our readers and our planet.
This book is made from Forest Stewardship Council® certified paper.